SHOW ME THE DATA!

SHOW ME THE DATA!

Data-Based Instructional Decisions Made Simple and Easy

RinaMarie Leon-Guerrero, Chris Matsumoto, and Jaime Martin
Experimental Education Unit
University of Washington

PUBLISHING
P.O. Box 23173
Shawnee Mission, Kansas 66283-0173
877-277-8254
www.aapcpublishing.net

© 2011 AAPC
P.O. Box 23173
Shawnee Mission, Kansas 66283-0173
www.aapcpublishing.net

Publisher's Cataloging-in-Publication

Leon-Guerrero, RinaMarie S.

Show me the data! : data-based instructional decisions made simple and easy / RinaMarie Leon-Guerrero, Chris Matsumoto, and Jaime Martin. -- Shawnee Mission, Kan. : Autism Asperger Pub. Co., c2011.

p. ; cm. + CD-ROM.

ISBN: 978-1-934575-73-4
LCCN: 2010941757

CD-ROM contains printable forms.

1. Autistic children--Education. 2. Autism spectrum disorders--Patients--Education. 3. Teachers of children with disabilities--Handbooks, manuals, etc. 4. Teaching--Aids and devices. I. Matsumoto, Chris (Chris Takeo), 1975- II. Martin, Jaime (Jaime Kay), 1980- III. Title.

LC4717.5 .L46 2011
371.94--dc22   1101

This book is designed in Helvetica Neue and AT Computer.

Printed in the United States of America.

ACKNOWLEDGMENTS

The collection of data sheets on the accompanying CD was developed by educators at the University of Washington's Experimental Education Unit (EEU) as a means of increasing the efficacy and efficiency of collecting data to monitor student progress.

We extend a special thank-you to all these educators for their efforts, contributions, and feedback to make *Show Me the Data!* a reality. We hope that these data sheets become an important part of your practice and that you have fun sharing the data with colleagues, parents, and team members for the benefit of your students and in compliance with the mandate for data-driven instruction.

TABLE OF CONTENTS

- **Adaptive**

- **Behavior**

- **Check-Off Charts**

- **Cognitive**

- **Communication**

- **General**

- **Motor**

- **Routines and Directions**

- **Social**

INTRODUCTION

The data sheets in this booklet and on the accompanying CD were designed to support teams in their efforts to systematically collect accurate information to make important decisions regarding intervention and instruction of students with disabilities. Data collection is one of the critical elements of an effective, efficient, and accountable program that supports student development and learning. Data form the basis for monitoring student progress, evaluating the effectiveness of instruction, determining the accuracy of programming, and collecting ongoing assessment information. Although the importance of data is very apparent, many intervention teams struggle to develop reasonable and sustainable methods of gathering information about student performance and progress.

Why Is Collecting Data So Difficult?

1. Teams face a lack of time and resources. Teams rarely have time to develop new data sheets for every Individualized Education Plan (IEP) or Individual Family Service Plan (IFSP) goal or outcome. And if they decide to use data sheets developed by someone else, there are few comprehensive collections of data sheets readily available.

   Show Me the Data! provides a comprehensive compilation of data sheets to assist teams in the careful and ongoing collection of information on student performance and progress across a diverse range of domains, ages, and abilities. The generic data sheets are appropriate for students of any age and/or ability, whereas the data sheets focusing on specific skills may be more appropriate for young children or children with significant cognitive delays. The majority of the data sheets allow providers and families to collect information through observation in a variety of settings and within the context of meaningful, developmentally appropriate activities.

2. Once teams have data sheets that are appropriate and easy to access, they often face a second obstacle. They must create a system that works for their particular program. Diversity in service delivery models, populations, professional disciplines, and frequency of intervention requires a certain level of customization of data sheets and the development of a system that meets the needs of staff members and families. The system must allow for easy maintenance and consistent data collection for all staff members. (Information is more meaningful when data are collected systematically and habitually.) Changes in students, especially the development of young children, can occur quickly, so data collection procedures must be responsive enough to capture the rapid growth and learning that can occur in a short period of time.

3. Even when teams have created systems to meet the unique needs of their organization and population, a third and very common problem is figuring out what to do with the data once they have been collected. When data are gathered using standard procedures and on a regular basis, the information can be displayed visually through graphs, enabling team members to make decisions more efficiently. In addition, the visual display of data allows interventionists and families to view the same information and use trends in the data during joint decision making. *Show Me the Data!* provides samples of completed data sheets and easy-to-use graphs that can serve as a model for teams to display their data visually and evaluate intervention effectiveness and program efficacy.

DATA COLLECTION IN THE CLASSROOM

Using evidence-based practices to teach children with disabilities is now more important than ever. Classroom teachers play an important part in evaluating the effectiveness of instructional programs for individual students. *Show Me the Data!* provides tools to make this easier in your classroom.

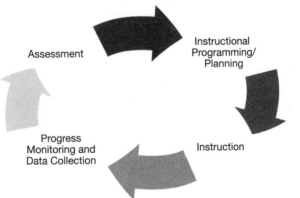

The above diagram shows the relation between assessment, instructional programming, instruction, and data collection. Each component directly influences the other. **Appropriate assessment** allows us to plan instruction on skills the student has not yet mastered. **Instructional programming** informs the **types of instruction** to be delivered. And, **data collection** allows us to make data-based instructional decisions to alter programming and instruction. The accompanying CD was designed to make the data collection more manageable by providing ready-to-use data sheets.

HOW TO USE THE DATA SHEETS

n addition to more general check-off charts, the accompanying CD contains a variety of data sheets targeting skills in the following domains:

- Adaptive

- Behavior

- Cognitive

- Communication

- General

- Motor

- Routines/Directions

- Social

How to Find the Data Sheet You Need on the CD

1. Determine which domain (e.g., ADAPTIVE, BEHAVIOR) a particular objective falls under; see also pages 27-30.

2. Open the chosen domain folder on the CD and choose a data sheet that is appropriate for the objective (see index file in each domain folder).

3. Files are labeled with a number as well as one of the following descriptors:
    S = Sample of applied use of form
    M = Modifiable version of form
    P = Print-only version of form
    For example, GENERAL_14S refers to a sample showing use of the data sheet on Interval Recording. GENERAL_14M refers to the same data sheet but blank and in modifiable form – the version you can customize on your computer. Finally, GENERAL_14P refers to the same data sheet but in print-only form – the version you print out and complete in handwriting if that is a better option for you and your team when collecting data.

CUSTOMIZING YOUR DATA SHEETS

It is our hope that the data sheets provided on the CD will be helpful to you in your classroom. However, we understand that you may need to customize them to fit you unique situation. That is why we have provided individual data sheets in several versions so you can complete them as electronic files or print them out and complete them in handwriting.

SETTING UP

There are many ways to collect data. Find what works best for your classroom. Once you get set up, your system will be easy to maintain.

Examples of Data Collection Systems

✐ Individual clipboards with pencils velcroed® or tied on for each child containing data sheets for each objective.

✐ Notebook containing the goals for one student or multiple students.

✐ Clipboard for each area (small group, free play, reading, etc.) listing all the students and their goals for the specific area.

We also encourage you to use the data sheets in the General section. **It is possible to take data on multiple children and/or behaviors on only ONE form.** It is important to consider, first and foremost, the efficacy of the data collection system. So, if using many different sheets is not effective, try using only one.

Be creative … rubber bands on your wrist, tape, counters in pocket!

Activity Matrix

🖊 An activity matrix is simply a table listing each child, his or her goals, and the times of the day at which instruction will be provided on those goals. Activity matrices are located in the General section.

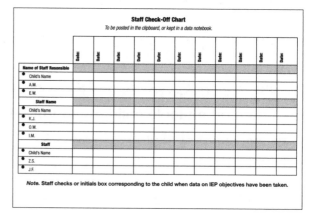

🖊 An activity matrix can serve multiple purposes. It can be used as a quick reference when planning activities, as a reference for other staff members, and even as a data sheet itself.

🖊 You can take data right on the activity matrix, which allows for an easy method of taking data on multiple children and objectives.

Keeping Data on Your Data

🖊 Check-off charts may be used to keep track of specific objectives on each child or to monitor overall data collection by staff. Utilizing a quick reference check-off chart can help teachers and staff remember what objectives to take data on.

🖊 Check-off charts can be posted on data clipboards, inside data notebooks, or posted in the classroom.

HELPFUL HINTS

Data Collection

⌀ Both an activity matrix and a check-off chart can be created as a simple table in any word processor, or you can use the ones provided here.

⌀ To take data, split data collection by specific objectives relevant to staff expertise. For example, the speech-language therapist takes all language data and the occupational/physical therapist takes gross-/fine-motor data.

⌀ Post frequently used data sheets on the wall, such as transition data sheets by the door and toileting data sheets in the bathroom.

⌀ Post staff check-off charts as reminders to ensure that data are being collected.

⌀ Most data sheets provide a general key for marking student performance based on level of prompting. You can use the key provided or use your own. However, it is important that a key is defined and used consistently to ensure accurate data collection.

Below are some keys commonly used throughout the data sheets. These are not an exhaustive list of all possible prompting strategies.

Key Sample 1: Prompting coded by abbreviations

I = Independent

G/V = Gestural/Verbal Prompt

PP = Partial Physical Prompt

FP = Full Physical Prompt

R = Resistance/Refusal

Key Sample 2: Prompting coded by number

0 = Resistance/Refusal

1 = Full Physical

2 = Partial Physical

3 = Verbal/Gestural Prompt

4 = Independent

TYPE OF PROMPT	DESCRIPTION	EXAMPLES
Gestural	Indicates to the child the correct answer by using a nonverbal response.	Pointing to the correct answer.
Verbal	Gives child additional verbal information to help him respond correctly.	Instruction was, "Clean up." You give the verbal prompt, "Put the blocks in the bucket."
Partial Physical	Partially physically touching the child in order to provide assistance.	Guiding a child to move his hands toward the sink to wash his hands by touching the child's elbow.
Full Physical	Physically touching the child to provide assistance in performing the desired response.	Physically guiding the child through the process of washing his hands by placing your hands over the child's hands.

SHOW ME THE DATA: NOW WHAT?

After individualized student goals have been identified and data have been collected, the next step is to use the data to make data-informed instructional decisions. In the following example, three students are profiled to demonstrate the ongoing flow from student objectives and planning for instruction (Parts 1 and 2) to collecting data on student performance (Part 3) to using data to make data-based instructional decisions (Part 4).

From Developing Student Learning Objectives to Monitoring Progress

Class Description

- Elementary school, K-5

- Special education resource room grades kindergarten through second grade

  - Mrs. Scott: special education teacher, full time

  - Mr. Lee: paraprofessional, part time

  - Ms. Ross: paraprofessional, part time

  - 10 students receiving specially designed instruction

  - Inclusion opportunities with limited paraprofessional support in the general education environment based on individual student strengths and needs

Part 1: Student Learning Goals

Child	Strengths	Needs	Emerging Skills	Goals/Objectives
Alec Kindergarten Interests include: • Listen to read-a-loud class stories • Music class • Peers	• At grade level for reading and math • Motivated by peers and social interaction • Maintains proximity to peers and observes social interaction	• Fine motor • Social interaction • Personal management of materials • Tolerating changes in routines	• Handwriting • Increasing conversations with peers • Following individual routines and directions • Increasing flexibility	• Write first name • Respond to peers and maintain cooperative play interaction • Follow group routines and directions • Accept change in routine and follow through with new routine
Jayden 1st Grade Interests: • Sports • Music and drumming • Adult answering his questions	• Gross-motor skills • Motivated by one-on-one adult interaction	• Performance below grade level in all academic areas; unable to sustain engagement in order to demonstrate skill and knowledge • Engagement in group activities • Appropriate gaining of adult attention (other than asking questions)	• Starting independent academic activities with adult one-on-one support • Picture identification • Counting up to 6 • Remaining engaged in activities • Verbally gain adult attention	• Maintain engagement in independent academic work • Identify letters • Maintain active engagement in small-group activities • Say person's name and make a comment to gain attention • Ask an adult for help
Alexa 2nd Grade Interests: • Reading and learning new languages • Drama and pretend play	• Above grade level in reading and language arts • Good organizational skills • Independent for all classroom routines	• Increased interest in peers • Social referencing • Math	• Cooperative play with peers • Recognizing emotions in others • Math computation with sums up to 30	• Join peers in play during recess and specialty activities • Read nonverbal cues and respond appropriately • Complete math computations with sums above 30

Part 2: Planning for Instruction

Activity Matrix for Mrs. Scott's Class

	Child: Alec	Child: Jayden	Child: Alexa
Routines and Transitions	• Respond to peer interaction • Follow group routines and directions • Accept change in routine and follow through with new routine	• Maintain active engagement in small-group activities	• Read nonverbal cues and respond appropriately
Fine Motor	• Write first name		
Gross Motor			
Social Communication	• Respond to peer interaction	• Say person's name and make a comment to gain attention • Ask an adult for help	• Read nonverbal cues and respond appropriately
Social Interactions	• Respond to peer interaction	• Say person's name and make a comment to gain attention	• Read nonverbal cues and respond appropriately • Join peers in play during recess and specialty activities
Reading	• Write first name • Follow group routines and directions	• Letter identification	
Math	• Write first name • Follow group routines and directions	• Maintain engagement in independent academic work • Request help from an adult	• Complete math computations with sums above 30
Science	• Write first name • Follow group routines and directions	• Maintain active engagement in small-group activities • Request help from an adult	
Language Arts	• Follow group routines and directions	• Maintain active engagement in small-group activities • Request help from an adult	
Specialties (Art, Computer, Music)	• Write first name • Accept change in routine and follow through with new routine	• Maintain engagement in independent academic work	• Join peers in play during recess and specialty activities

Part 3: Collecting Data to Monitor Student Progress

Below are two examples of using data sheets to collect data on Alec's objectives. The first example demonstrates using a group data sheet, and the second example demonstrates using individual data sheets.

Example 1: Using a group data sheet to collect data on multiple objectives. Featured are data sheets for three days.

Date: February 7

Alec					Jayden				Alexa				Student 4			
Goal 1: Write first name					Goal 1: Maintain active engagement in small-group activities				Goal 1: Join peers in play during recess and specialty activities				Goal 1:			
Trials:					Trials:				Trials:				Trials:			
P	P	P	P													
Goal 2: Respond to peer and maintain interaction					Goal 2: Maintain active engagement in independent academic work				Goal 2: Read nonverbal cues and respond appropriately				Goal 2:			
Activity: *Board Game 7 Min*					Trials:				Trials:				Trials:			
P																
Goal 3: Follow group and routine directions					Goal 3: Identify letter				Goal 3: Complete math computations with sums above 30				Goal 3:			
Trials:					Trials:				Trials:				Trials:			
P	P	I	I	P												
P	P	P	P	P												
Goal 4: Accept change in routine and follow through with new routine					Goal 4: Request help from an adult				Goal 4:				Goal 4:			
Trials:					Trials:				Trials:				Trials:			
P	P															

Date: February 11

Alec	Jayden	Alexa	Student 4
Goal 1: Write first name	Goal 1: Maintain active engagement in small-group activities	Goal 1: Join peers in play during recess and specialty activities	Goal 1:
Trials:	Trials:	Trials:	Trials:
P | P | P | – | –			
Goal 2: Respond to peer and maintain interaction	Goal 2: Maintain active engagement in independent academic work	Goal 2: Read nonverbal cues and responding appropriately	Goal 2:
Activity: *Board Game 9 Min*	Trials:	Trials:	Trials:
P			
Goal 3: Follow group and routine directions	Goal 3: Identify letter	Goal 3: Complete math computations with sums above 30	Goal 3:
Trials:	Trials:	Trials:	Trials:
I | I | I | P | P P | P | P | I | P			
Goal 4: Accept change in routine and follow through with new routine	Goal 4: Request help from an adult	Goal 4:	Goal 4:
Trials:	Trials:	Trials:	Trials:
I			

Date: February 17

Alec	Jayden	Alexa	Student 4
Goal 1: Write first name	Goal 1: Maintain active engagement in small-group activities	Goal 1: Join peers in play during recess and specialty activities	Goal 1:
Trials:	Trials:	Trials:	Trials:
P | P | R | R | P			
Goal 2: Respond to peer and maintain interaction	Goal 2: Maintain active engagement in independent academic work	Goal 2: Read nonverbal cues and respond appropriately	Goal 2:
Activity: *Board Game 7 Min*	Trials:	Trials:	Trials:
P			
Goal 3: Follow group and routine directions	Goal 3: Identify letter	Goal 3: Complete math computations with sums above 30	Goal 3:
Trials:	Trials:	Trials:	Trials:
Goal 4: Accept change in routine and follow through with new routine	Goal 4: Request help from an adult	Goal 4:	Goal 4:
Trials:	Trials:	Trials:	Trials:

Example 2: Using individual data sheets for each objective. Featured are four data sheets for four separate objectives. Each sheet spans multiple days.

Name: Alec

Objective: Write first name

Criteria:

Date	Trial 1	Trial 2	Trial 3	Trial 4	Trial 5
Motor Skills					
DATE: 2/7	I G/V PP (FP) R	I G/V PP (FP) R	I G/V (PP) FP R	I G/V (PP) FP R	I G/V PP FP R
DATE: 2/11	I G/V (PP) FP R	I G/V (PP) FP R	I G/V PP (FP) R	I G/V PP FP (R)	I G/V PP FP (R)
DATE: 2/14	I G/V PP FP (R)	I G/V PP (FP) R	I G/V PP FP (R)	I G/V PP (FP) R	I G/V PP FP R
DATE: 2/15	I G/V PP (FP) R	I G/V PP (FP) R	I G/V PP (FP) R	I G/V PP FP (R)	I G/V PP (FP) R
DATE: 2/17	I G/V PP (FP) R	I G/V PP (FP) R	I G/V PP FP (R)	I G/V PP FP (R)	I G/V PP (FP) R

Key:

I = Independent   G/V = Gestural/Verbal   PP = Partial Physical Assistance   FP = Full Partial Assistance   R = Refusal

18

Name: Alec

Objective: Respond to peer and maintain cooperative play interaction

Criteria:

Date	Play Activity	Prompting	Minutes Engaged in Play		Date	Play Activity	Prompting	Minutes Engaged in Play
2/7	Board game	I G/V (PP) FP R	7				I G/V PP FP R	
2/8	Blocks	I G/V (PP) FP R	10				I G/V PP FP R	
2/10	Chase – Recess	I G/V PP (FP) R	5				I G/V PP FP R	
2/11	Board game	I G/V (PP) FP R	9				I G/V PP FP R	
2/14	Blocks	I G/V (PP) FP R	8				I G/V PP FP R	
2/15	Arts and crafts	I G/V PP (FP) R	6				I G/V PP FP R	
2/17	Arts and crafts	I G/V PP (FP) R	7				I G/V PP FP R	
2/21	Red Light – Recess	I G/V (PP) FP R	7				I G/V PP FP R	
2/23	Legos	I (G/V) PP FP R	10				I G/V PP FP R	
2/24	Puzzles	I (G/V) PP FP R	12				I G/V PP FP R	
		I G/V PP FP R					I G/V PP FP R	
		I G/V PP FP R					I G/V PP FP R	
		I G/V PP FP R					I G/V PP FP R	

Key:

I = Independent   G/V = Gestural/Verbal   PP = Partial Physical Assistance   FP = Full Partial Assistance   R = Refusal

Show Me the Data!

Name: Alec

Objective: Follow group routines and directions

Criteria:

Key:
0 = Refusal
1 = Full Physical
2 = Partial Physical
3 = Verbal/Gestural Prompt
4 = Independent

Date: Feb 7

Activity	0	1	Level of Assistance 2	3	4
Arrival	0	1	**(2)**	3	4
Calendar	0	1	**(2)**	3	4
Reading	0	1	2	3	**(4)**
Recess	0	1	2	3	**(4)**
Math	0	1	**(2)**	3	4
Lunch	0	1	2	**(3)**	4
PE	0	**(1)**	2	3	4
Choice	0	1	**(2)**	3	4
Snack	0	1	**(2)**	3	4
Pack Up	0	1	**(2)**	3	4

Date: Feb 8

Activity	0	1	Level of Assistance 2	3	4
Arrival	0	1	**(2)**	3	**(4)**
Calendar	0	1	**(2)**	3	**(4)**
Reading	0	1	2	3	**(4)**
Recess	0	1	2	**(3)**	4
Math	0	**(1)**	2	3	4
Lunch	0	1	**(2)**	3	**(4)**
PE	0	1	2	3	**(4)**
Choice	0	1	**(2)**	3	**(4)**
Snack	0	1	2	3	**(4)**
Pack Up	0	1	2	3	**(4)**

Date: Feb 9

Activity	0	1	Level of Assistance 2	3	4
Arrival	0	**(1)**	2	3	4
Calendar	0	**(1)**	2	3	4
Reading	0	1	2	**(3)**	4
Recess	0	**(1)**	2	3	4
Math	0	**(1)**	2	3	4
Lunch	0	1	**(2)**	3	4
PE	0	**(1)**	2	3	4
Choice	0	**(1)**	2	3	4
Snack	0	1	**(2)**	3	4
Pack Up	0	1	**(2)**	3	4

Date: Feb 10

Activity	0	1	Level of Assistance 2	3	4
Arrival	0	1	**(2)**	3	4
Calendar	0	1	**(2)**	3	4
Reading	0	1	2	3	**(4)**
Recess	0	**(1)**	2	3	4
Math	0	**(1)**	2	3	4
Lunch	0	1	**(2)**	3	4
PE	0	**(1)**	2	3	4
Choice	0	**(1)**	2	3	4
Snack	0	1	**(2)**	3	4
Pack Up	0	1	**(2)**	3	4

Date: Feb 11

Activity	0	1	Level of Assistance 2	3	4
Arrival	0	1	2	3	**(4)**
Calendar	0	1	2	3	**(4)**
Reading	0	1	2	3	**(4)**
Recess	0	1	2	**(3)**	4
Math	0	1	2	3	4
Lunch	0	1	2	**(3)**	4
PE	0	1	**(2)**	3	4
Choice	0	1	2	**(3)**	4
Snack	0	1	**(2)**	3	4
Pack Up	0	1	2	3	4

Name: Alec	
Objective: Accept change in routine and follow through with new routine	**Criteria:**

Date	**Activity/Transition**	**Response to Cue**
2/7	School early release	I ⊛G/V PP FP R
2/7	Eat school lunch	I G/V PP ⊛FP R
2/8	Move to new reading group	I G/V ⊛PP FP R
2/9	Math group with substitute teacher	I G/V ⊛PP FP R
2/10	Fieldtrip	I ⊛G/V PP FP R
2/11	New game in PE	⊛I G/V PP FP R
2/12	Eat school lunch	⊛I G/V PP FP R
2/12	Fire Drill	⊛I G/V PP FP R
2/13	Eat new food item in lunch	⊛I G/V PP FP R
		I G/V PP FP R
		I G/V PP FP R
		I G/V PP FP R
		I G/V PP FP R
		I G/V PP FP R
		I G/V PP FP R
		I G/V PP FP R
		I G/V PP FP R

Key:
I = Independent
G/V = Gestural/Verbal
PP = Partial Physical Assistance
FP = Full Physical Assistance
R = Refusal

Part 4: Reviewing Data to Make Data-Informed Instructional Decisions

Featured below are graphs generated from the data collected for Alec's objectives. Visually displaying the data provides an easy format for analysis and making instructional decisions.

Objective 1: Write own name

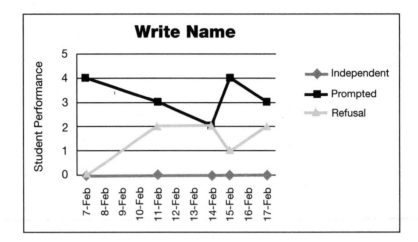

Data-based decision: Alec is not making progress on this goal. Program should CHANGE instruction, task, or reinforcement.

Objective 2: Respond to peer and maintain cooperative play interactions

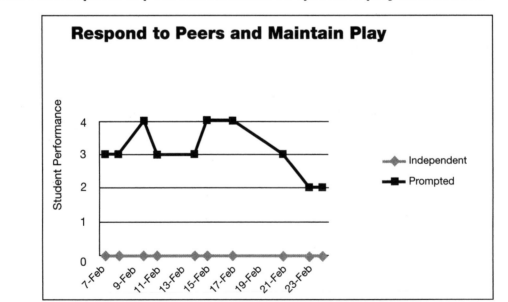

Data-based decision: Alec is making progress on this goal. He is requiring less intrusive prompts to respond to peers and maintain play. Program should STAY.

Objective 3: Follow group routines and directions

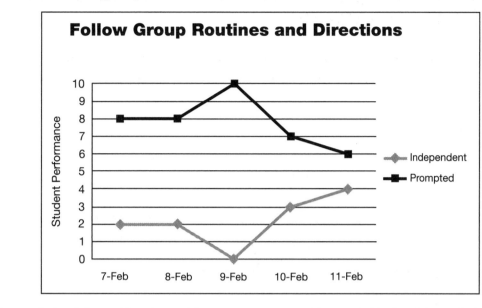

Data-based decision: Alec is making progress on this goal. He is able to follow routines more independently. Program should STAY.

Objective 4: Accept change in routine and follow through with new routine

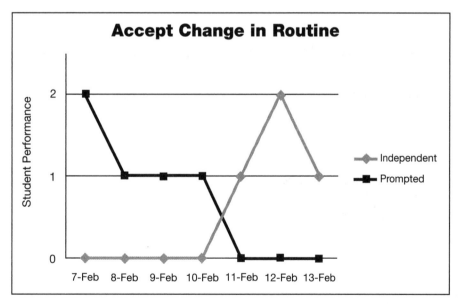

Data-based decision: Alec is making progress on this goal. He is able to independently accept changes in routine. Program should MOVE ON.

TRY IT!

After this general introduction to data collection, and in particular the data sheets presented in the following pages and on the accompanying CD, it is now time for you to try it out. We are confident that you will soon find that the often-dreaded task of collecting data can easily be integrated into your daily routines without causing an undue burden on you or any other member of the instructional team.

The reality is: You must collect data to ensure high-quality instruction and the best possible outcome for your students. The information presented here and the comprehensive set of data sheets on the accompanying CD will make your task less time-consuming and more efficient. Finally, don't forget – individual data sheets are easily tweaked and adjusted depending upon your instructional situation and your students' needs.

Good Luck!

DATA SHEETS BY DOMAIN

ITEM	FILE NAME
ADAPTIVE	
Daily Eating Record – One Week	ADAPTIVE_1M, ADAPTIVE_1P
Daily Toileting Schedule	ADAPTIVE_2M, ADAPTIVE_2P
Drinking	ADAPTIVE_3M, ADAPTIVE_3P
Eating	ADAPTIVE_4M, ADAPTIVE_4P
Feeding	ADAPTIVE_5M, ADAPTIVE_5P
Hand Washing	ADAPTIVE_6M, ADAPTIVE_6P
Pouring	ADAPTIVE_7M, ADAPTIVE_7P
Putting on Coat	ADAPTIVE_8M, ADAPTIVE_8P
Removing Coat/Backpack	ADAPTIVE_9M, ADAPTIVE_9P
Snack	ADAPTIVE_10M, ADAPTIVE_10P
Toileting Routine	ADAPTIVE_11M, ADAPTIVE_11P
Utensil Use	ADAPTIVE_12M, ADAPTIVE_12P
Weekly Potty Training Record	ADAPTIVE_13M, ADAPTIVE_13P
BEHAVIOR	
A-B-C	BEHAVIOR_1M, BEHAVIOR_1P
A-B-C-2	BEHAVIOR_2M, BEHAVIOR_2P
Behavior Likert Scale – Sample	BEHAVIOR_3S
Behavior Likert Scale	BEHAVIOR_3M, BEHAVIOR_3P
Behavior Observation Form	BEHAVIOR_4M, BEHAVIOR_4P
Behavioral Program	BEHAVIOR_5M, BEHAVIOR_5P
Duration Recording	BEHAVIOR_6M, BEHAVIOR_6P
Frequency Data	BEHAVIOR_7M, BEHAVIOR_7P
Scatterplot – Sample	BEHAVIOR_8S
Scatterplot	BEHAVIOR_8M, BEHAVIOR_8P
CHECK-OFF CHARTS	
Data Check-Off Chart	CHECK_1M, CHECK_1P
Staff Check-Off Chart	CHECK_2M, CHECK_2P

COGNITIVE	
Basic Shapes	COGNITIVE_1M
Basic Shapes – blank to create own	COGNITIVE_1P
Blending Sounds	COGNITIVE_2M, COGNITIVE_2P
Body Parts	COGNITIVE_3M, COGNITIVE_3P
Choice Making	COGNITIVE_4M, COGNITIVE_4P
Colors	COGNITIVE_5M, COGNITIVE_5P
Completing Activities	COGNITIVE_6M, COGNITIVE_6P
Completing Multistep Task	COGNITIVE_7M, COGNITIVE_7P
Concepts	COGNITIVE_8M, COGNITIVE_8P
Counting 1-10	COGNITIVE_9M, COGNITIVE_9P
Letters of the Alphabet – Recognition	COGNITIVE_10M, COGNITIVE_10P
Letters of the Alphabet – Sounds	COGNITIVE_11M, COGNITIVE_11P
Matching	COGNITIVE_12M, COGNITIVE_12P
Sequencing Story	COGNITIVE_13M, COGNITIVE_13P
Sound-Symbol Correspondence	COGNITIVE_14M, COGNITIVE_14P
Specific Directions	COGNITIVE_15M, COGNITIVE_15P
COMMUNICATION	
Articulation	COMM_1M, COMM_1P
Asking/Answering Questions	COMM_2M, COMM_2P
Communicative Exchanges	COMM_3M, COMM_3P
Communicative Initiations	COMM_4M, COMM_4P
Ending Conversations	COMM_5M, COMM_5P
Expressive Vocabulary	COMM_6M, COMM_6P
Expressive Word List	COMM_7M, COMM_7P
Gain Partner's Attention	COMM_8M, COMM_8P
Identifying Familiar People	COMM_9M, COMM_9P
Oral-Motor Imitation	COMM_10M, COMM_10P
Receptive Word List	COMM_11M, COMM_11P
Reciprocal Response	COMM_12M, COMM_12P
Respond to Name	COMM_13M, COMM_13P
GENERAL	
5 Trial	GENERAL_1M, GENERAL_1P
Activity Matrix – Sample	GENERAL_2S

Data Sheets by Domain

Activity Matrix	GENERAL_2M, GENERAL_2P
Activity Matrix for Preschool/Kindergarten Classroom	GENERAL_3M, GENERAL_3P
Activity Matrix for a Play Date	GENERAL_4M, GENERAL_4P
Activity Matrix for a Social Skills Group	GENERAL_5M, GENERAL_5P
Anecdotal Record	GENERAL_6M, GENERAL_6P
Basic Prompting 0-4	GENERAL_7M, GENERAL_7P
Daily Data Sheet – Sample	GENERAL_8S
Daily Data Sheet	GENERAL_8M, GENERAL_8P
Data by Activity – Multiple Students (1) – Sample	GENERAL_9S
Data by Activity – Multiple Students (1)	GENERAL_9M, GENERAL_9P
Data by Activity – Multiple Students (2) – Sample	GENERAL_10S
Data by Activity – Multiple Students (2)	GENERAL_10M, GENERAL_10P
Data by Number Amount	GENERAL_11M, GENERAL_11P
Data by Student Multiple Objectives – Sample	GENERAL_12S
Data by Student Multiple Objectives	GENERAL_12M, GENERAL_12P
Free-Choice Data Matrix – Sample	GENERAL_13S
Free-Choice Data Matrix	GENERAL_13M, GENERAL_13P
Interval Recording – Sample	GENERAL_14S
Interval Recording	GENERAL_14M, GENERAL_14P
Likert Scale – Sample	GENERAL_15S
Likert Scale	GENERAL_15M, GENERAL_15P
Mass Trials	GENERAL_16M, GENERAL_16P
Outcome or Objective Update	GENERAL_17M, GENERAL_17P
Repeated Trials – Sample	GENERAL_18S
Repeated Trials	GENERAL_18M, GENERAL_18P

MOTOR	
Balance Beam	MOTOR_1M, MOTOR_1P
Copying	MOTOR_2M, MOTOR_2P
General Motor Imitation	MOTOR_3M, MOTOR_3P
Motor Skills – 1	MOTOR_4M, MOTOR_4P
Motor Skills – 2 – Sample	MOTOR_5S
Motor Skills – 2	MOTOR_5M, MOTOR_5P
Using Scissors	MOTOR_6M, MOTOR_6P

ROUTINES AND DIRECTIONS	
Arrival/Dismissal Directions	ROU_DIR_1M, ROU_DIR_1P
Directive Commands	ROU_DIR_2M, ROU_DIR_2P
Following Directions	ROU_DIR_3M, ROU_DIR_3P
Response to Transition Cue	ROU_DIR_4M, ROU_DIR_4P
Routine/Transitions	ROU_DIR_5M, ROU_DIR_5P
Two-Step Directions	ROU_DIR_6M, ROU_DIR_6P
SOCIAL	
Accepting Items from Peers	SOCIAL_1M, SOCIAL_1P
Combined Data Collection and Matrix – Sample	SOCIAL_2S
Combined Data Collection and Matrix	SOCIAL_2M, SOCIAL_2P
Cooperative Play	SOCIAL_3M, SOCIAL_3P
Sharing	SOCIAL_4M, SOCIAL_4P
Turn-Taking	SOCIAL_5M, SOCIAL_5P

ADAPTIVE

Daily Eating Record – One Week

		Date:
Staff:		

Name:

Objective:

Criteria:

Date	Offered at AM Snack	Offered at Lunch	Offered at PM Snack	Food Consumed/Comments
MON				
TUES				
WED				
THUR				
FRI				

Show Me the Data! By Leon-Guerrero, Matsumoto, & Martin © 2011. AAPC. www.aapcpublishing.net
ADAPTIVE – Daily Eating Record – One Week

Daily Toileting Schedule

Staff: **Date:**

Name:

Objective:

Criteria:

Dates

Time																		

Record response using key.

Key:

D = Dry

Student Initiated
U+ = Urinate on Toilet
B+ = BM on Toilet
D+ = No Urination or BM

Teacher Assisted
U- = Urinate on Toilet
B- = BM on Toilet
D- = No Urination or BM

Accidents
w = Wet Pants
b = BM in Pants

Show Me the Data! By Leon-Guerrero, Matsumoto, & Martin © 2011. AAPC. www.aapcpublishing.net
ADAPTIVE – Daily Toileting Schedule

Drinking

Staff:

Date:

Name:

Objective:

Criteria:

Date	Level of Assistance	Spillage: Yes/No	Amount Consumed	Comments
	4 3 2 1 0	YES / NO		
	4 3 2 1 0	YES / NO		
	4 3 2 1 0	YES / NO		
	4 3 2 1 0	YES / NO		
	4 3 2 1 0	YES / NO		
	4 3 2 1 0	YES / NO		
	4 3 2 1 0	YES / NO		

Circle response using key.

Key:

4 = Independent   3 = Verbal/Gestural   2 = Partial Physical   1 = Full Physical   0 = Refusal

Show Me the Data! By Leon-Guerrero, Matsumoto, & Martin © 2011. AAPC. www.aapcpublishing.net
ADAPTIVE – Drinking

Eating

Staff:	Date:

Name:	
Objective:	
Criteria:	

Date:					**Date:**			
Amount Served/Food Type:					**Amount Served/Food Type:**			
Amount Consumed:					**Amount Consumed:**			
Comments:					**Comments:**			

Feeding

	Staff:	Date:
Name:		
Objective:		
Criteria:		

Date: _____

Amount Served: _____

Amount Consumed: _____

Reinforcement Used: _____

Comments: _____

_____

_____

Date: _____

Amount Served: _____

Amount Consumed: _____

Reinforcement Used: _____

Comments: _____

_____

_____

Date: _____

Amount Served: _____

Amount Consumed: _____

Reinforcement Used: _____

Comments: _____

_____

_____

Date: _____

Amount Served: _____

Amount Consumed: _____

Reinforcement Used: _____

Comments: _____

_____

_____

Hand Washing

Name:		Staff:		Date:
Objective:				
Criteria:				

Date:

Trial	1	2	3	4	5	6	7	8	9	10
	Turn on water	Wet hands	Put soap onto hands	Rub hands back and forth	Rinse	Turn off water	Get Paper Towel	Dry hands	Throw towel in trash	
Student Response	I G/V PP FP R	I G/V PP FP R	I G/V PP FP R	I G/V PP FP R	I G/V PP FP R	I G/V PP FP R	I G/V PP FP R	I G/V PP FP R	I G/V PP FP R	I G/V PP FP R

Date:

Trial	1	2	3	4	5	6	7	8	9	10
	Turn on water	Wet hands	Put soap onto hands	Rub hands back and forth	Rinse	Turn off water	Get Paper Towel	Dry hands	Throw towel in trash	
Student Response	I G/V PP FP R	I G/V PP FP R	I G/V PP FP R	I G/V PP FP R	I G/V PP FP R	I G/V PP FP R	I G/V PP FP R	I G/V PP FP R	I G/V PP FP R	I G/V PP FP R

Date:

Trial	1	2	3	4	5	6	7	8	9	10
	Turn on water	Wet hands	Put soap onto hands	Rub hands back and forth	Rinse	Turn off water	Get Paper Towel	Dry hands	Throw towel in trash	
Student Response	I G/V PP FP R	I G/V PP FP R	I G/V PP FP R	I G/V PP FP R	I G/V PP FP R	I G/V PP FP R	I G/V PP FP R	I G/V PP FP R	I G/V PP FP R	I G/V PP FP R

Circle response using key.

Key:

I = Independent   G/V = Gestural/Verbal Prompt   PP = Partial Physical Prompt   FP = Full Physical Prompt   R = Resistance/Refusal

Show Me the Data! By Leon-Guerrero, Matsumoto, & Martin © 2011. AAPC. www.aapcpublishing.net

ADAPTIVE – Hand Washing

Pouring

Staff: _____ **Date:** _____

Name: _____

Objective: _____

Criteria: _____

Date:	Level of Assistance:	Pouring From:	Pouring To:
Comments:			

Date:	Level of Assistance:	Pouring From:	Pouring To:
Comments:			

Date:	Level of Assistance:	Pouring From:	Pouring To:
Comments:			

Date:	Level of Assistance:	Pouring From:	Pouring To:
Comments:			

Date:	Level of Assistance:	Pouring From:	Pouring To:
Comments:			

Date:	Level of Assistance:	Pouring From:	Pouring To:
Comments:			

Record level of assistance using key.

Key:

I = Independent   G/V = Gestural/Verbal Prompt   PP = Partial Physical Prompt   FP = Full Physical Prompt   R = Resistance/Refusal

Show Me the Data! By Leon-Guerrero, Matsumoto, & Martin © 2011. AAPC. www.aapcpublishing.net
ADAPTIVE – Pouring

Putting on Coat

Staff:	Date:

Name:

Objective:

Criteria:

Date:

Trial	1	2	3	4	5
	Get coat off of hook	Put on coat	Fasten fasteners (snaps, buttons, zipper)		
Assistance	I G/V PP FP R	I G/V PP FP R	I G/V PP FP R	I G/V PP FP R	I G/V PP FP R

Date:

Trial	1	2	3	4	5
	Get coat off of hook	Put on coat	Fasten fasteners (snaps, buttons, zipper)		
Assistance	I G/V PP FP R	I G/V PP FP R	I G/V PP FP R	I G/V PP FP R	I G/V PP FP R

Date:

Trial	1	2	3	4	5
	Get coat off of hook	Put on coat	Fasten fasteners (snaps, buttons, zipper)		
Assistance	I G/V PP FP R	I G/V PP FP R	I G/V PP FP R	I G/V PP FP R	I G/V PP FP R

Circle response using key.

Key:

I = Independent   G/V = Gestural/Verbal Prompt   PP = Partial Physical Prompt   FP = Full Physical Prompt   R = Resistance/Refusal

Show Me the Data! By Leon-Guerrero, Matsumoto, & Martin © 2011. AAPC. www.aapcpublishing.net
ADAPTIVE – Putting on Coat

Removing Coat/Backpack

Name:

Objective:

Criteria:

Staff: Date:

Date:

Trial	1	2	3	4	5
	Unfasten coat	Remove coat	Hang coat on hook	Remove backpack	Hang backpack on hook
Assistance	I G/V PP FP R	I G/V PP FP R	I G/V PP FP R	I G/V PP FP R	I G/V PP FP R

Date:

Trial	1	2	3	4	5
	Unfasten coat	Remove coat	Hang coat on hook	Remove backpack	Hang backpack on hook
Assistance	I G/V PP FP R	I G/V PP FP R	I G/V PP FP R	I G/V PP FP R	I G/V PP FP R

Date:

Trial	1	2	3	4	5
	Unfasten coat	Remove coat	Hang coat on hook	Remove backpack	Hang backpack on hook
Assistance	I G/V PP FP R	I G/V PP FP R	I G/V PP FP R	I G/V PP FP R	I G/V PP FP R

Circle response using key.

Key:

I = Independent   G/V = Gestural/Verbal Prompt   PP = Partial Physical Prompt   FP = Full Physical Prompt   R = Resistance/Refusal

Show Me the Data! By Leon-Guerrero, Matsumoto, & Martin © 2011. AAPC. www.aapcpublishing.net
ADAPTIVE – Removing Coat/Backpack

Snack

Name:

Objective:

Criteria:

Staff: **Date:**

Objective	Date	+/-	Food Type (if applicable)	Amount Consumed (if applicable)	Comments/Anecdotal Notes
Use fork or spoon					
Drink					
Eat					
Pouring					

Objective	Date	+/-	Food Type (if applicable)	Amount Consumed (if applicable)	Comments/Anecdotal Notes
Use fork or spoon					
Drink					
Eat					
Pouring					

Key:
Use +/- to record presence or absence of response.

Show Me the Data! By Leon-Guerrero, Matsumoto, & Martin © 2011. AAPC. www.aapcpublishing.net
ADAPTIVE – Snack

Toileting Routine

Staff: _____ **Date:** _____

Name: _____

Objective: _____

Criteria: _____

Date: _____

Trial	1	2	3	4	5	6	7	8	9	10
	Go into bathroom	Pull pants down	Eliminate	Flush	Pull pants up	Fasten clothing	Wash hands	Dry hands	Throw towel in trash	
Assistance	I G/V PP FP R	I G/V PP FP R	I G/V PP FP R	I G/V PP FP R	I G/V PP FP R	I G/V PP FP R	I G/V PP FP R	I G/V PP FP R	I G/V PP FP R	I G/V PP FP R

Date: _____

Trial	1	2	3	4	5	6	7	8	9	10
	Go into bathroom	Pull pants down	Eliminate	Flush	Pull pants up	Fasten clothing	Wash hands	Dry hands	Throw towel in trash	
Assistance	I G/V PP FP R	I G/V PP FP R	I G/V PP FP R	I G/V PP FP R	I G/V PP FP R	I G/V PP FP R	I G/V PP FP R	I G/V PP FP R	I G/V PP FP R	I G/V PP FP R

Date: _____

Trial	1	2	3	4	5	6	7	8	9	10
	Go into bathroom	Pull pants down	Eliminate	Flush	Pull pants up	Fasten clothing	Wash hands	Dry hands	Throw towel in trash	
Assistance	I G/V PP FP R	I G/V PP FP R	I G/V PP FP R	I G/V PP FP R	I G/V PP FP R	I G/V PP FP R	I G/V PP FP R	I G/V PP FP R	I G/V PP FP R	I G/V PP FP R

Circle response using key.

Key:

I = Independent   G/V = Gestural/Verbal Prompt   PP = Partial Physical Prompt   FP = Full Physical Prompt   R = Resistance/Refusal

Show Me the Data! By Leon-Guerrero, Matsumoto, & Martin © 2011. AAPC. www.aapcpublishing.net

ADAPTIVE – Toileting Routine

Utensil Use

Staff: _____ **Date:** _____

Name: _____

Objective: _____

Criteria: _____

Utensil: _____

Date	Type of Food	Child Initiated	Spillage	Comments
		YES/NO	YES/NO	

Utensil: _____

Date	Type of Food	Child Initiated	Spillage	Comments
		YES/NO	YES/NO	

Utensil: _____

Date	Type of Food	Child Initiated	Spillage	Comments
		YES/NO	YES/NO	

Utensil: _____

Date	Type of Food	Child Initiated	Spillage	Comments
		YES/NO	YES/NO	

Utensil: _____

Date	Type of Food	Child Initiated	Spillage	Comments
		YES/NO	YES/NO	

Record response by circling Yes or No.

Show Me the Data! By Leon-Guerrero, Matsumoto, & Martin © 2011. AAPC. www.aapcpublishing.net
ADAPTIVE – Utensil Use

Weekly Potty Training Record

Name:		Staff:		Date:
Objective:				
Criteria:				

	6am	7	8	9	10	11	12pm	1	2	3	4	5	6	7	8	9	night
Mon																	
Tues																	
Wed																	
Thurs																	
Fri																	
Sat																	
Sun																	

Record response using key.

Key:

D = Dry

Student Initiated
U+ = Urinate on Toilet
B+ = BM on Toilet
D+ = No Urination or BM

Teacher Assisted
U- = Urinate on Toilet
B- = BM on Toilet
D- = No Urination or BM

Accidents
w = Wet Pants
b = BM in Pants

BEHAVIOR

ABC

Name:			Staff:		Date:
Teacher:		Date(s):			

Antecedent to Behavior	Behavior (Describe in a Measurable Way)	Consequence to Behavior

ABC-2

Staff: _____ **Date:** _____

Student Name: _____

Date and Time:	
Antecedent: (What was happening right before the behavior?)	
Behavior: (State as specifically as possible)	
Consequence: (Exactly what you did and how student reacted)	
Other: State any other observations you think might be useful (e.g., possible setting events that might have affected situation).	

Date and Time:	
Antecedent: (What was happening right before the behavior?)	
Behavior: (State as specifically as possible)	
Consequence: (Exactly what you did and how student reacted)	
Other: State any other observations you think might be useful (e.g., possible setting events that might have affected situation)	

Behavior Likert Scale – Sample

Week of:

Staff: Smith   **Date:** 5/11/10

Activity	Monday (Circle one number)	Tuesday (Circle one number)	Wednesday (Circle one number)	Thursday (Circle one number)	Friday (Circle one number)
Journal	0 1 (2) 3	0 (1) 2 3	0 (1) 2 3	0 1 (2) 3	0 1 2 (3)
Snack	(0) 1 2 3	(0) 1 2 3	(0) 1 2 3	(0) 1 2 3	(0) 1 2 3
Circle	(0) 1 2 3	0 1 (2) 3	0 (1) 2 3	0 (1) 2 3	(0) 1 2 3
Reading	0 1 2 (3)	0 1 (2) 3	0 1 2 (3)	0 1 (2) 3	0 1 2 (3)
Recess	(0) 1 2 3	0 (1) 2 3	0 1 (2) 3	0 1 (2) 3	0 (1) 2 3
Math	0 1 2 (3)	0 1 2 (3)	0 1 (2) 3	0 1 (2) 3	0 1 2 (3)
Lunch/Recess	(0) 1 2 3	0 (1) 2 3	0 1 (2) 3	0 (1) 2 3	0 (1) 2 3
Small Group	0 1 2 (3)	0 1 2 (3)	0 1 (2) 3	0 1 2 (3)	0 1 2 (3)
Choice Time	0 1 2 (3)	0 1 (2) 3	0 1 (2) 3	0 1 (2) 3	0 1 2 (3)
Snack	(0) 1 2 3	(0) 1 2 3	(0) 1 2 3	(0) 1 2 3	(0) 1 2 3
Recess	(0) 1 2 3	0 (1) 2 3	(0) 1 2 3	(0) 1 2 3	(0) 1 2 3
Shared Reading	0 1 2 (3)	0 1 (2) 3	0 1 2 (3)	0 1 2 (3)	0 1 (2) 3
Bus	(0) 1 2 3	(0) 1 2 3	(0) 1 2 3	(0) 1 2 3	(0) 1 2 3
Average Score:	Average 33/17 = 2	Average 33/18 = 2	Average 33/18 = 2	Average 33/18 = 2	Average 33/19 = 2

Use the key below to qualify the behavior, ranging from 0, which would be no occurrence, to 3, which is the most severe.

Key:

0 = _____   1 = _____   2 = _____   3 = _____

Example: for outbursts and aggression: 0 = No problems; 1= Whining, resisting; 2 = Screaming; 3 = Screaming, hitting, other aggression

Show Me the Data! By Leon-Guerrero, Matsumoto, & Martin © 2011. AAPC. www.aapcpublishing.net
BEHAVIOR – Behavior Likert Scale – Sample

Behavior Likert Scale

Staff:	Date:

Week of:

Activity	Monday (Circle one number)	Tuesday (Circle one number)	Wednesday (Circle one number)	Thursday (Circle one number)	Friday (Circle one number)
	0 1 2 3	0 1 2 3	0 1 2 3	0 1 2 3	0 1 2 3
	0 1 2 3	0 1 2 3	0 1 2 3	0 1 2 3	0 1 2 3
	0 1 2 3	0 1 2 3	0 1 2 3	0 1 2 3	0 1 2 3
	0 1 2 3	0 1 2 3	0 1 2 3	0 1 2 3	0 1 2 3
	0 1 2 3	0 1 2 3	0 1 2 3	0 1 2 3	0 1 2 3
	0 1 2 3	0 1 2 3	0 1 2 3	0 1 2 3	0 1 2 3
	0 1 2 3	0 1 2 3	0 1 2 3	0 1 2 3	0 1 2 3
	0 1 2 3	0 1 2 3	0 1 2 3	0 1 2 3	0 1 2 3
	0 1 2 3	0 1 2 3	0 1 2 3	0 1 2 3	0 1 2 3
	0 1 2 3	0 1 2 3	0 1 2 3	0 1 2 3	0 1 2 3
	0 1 2 3	0 1 2 3	0 1 2 3	0 1 2 3	0 1 2 3
	0 1 2 3	0 1 2 3	0 1 2 3	0 1 2 3	0 1 2 3
	0 1 2 3	0 1 2 3	0 1 2 3	0 1 2 3	0 1 2 3
Average Score:	Average _____	Average _____	Average _____	Average _____	Average _____

Use the key below to qualify the behavior, ranging from 0, which would be no occurrence, to 3, which is the most severe.

Key:

0 = _____   1 = _____   2 = _____   3 = _____

Example: for outbursts and aggression: 0 = No problems; 1 = Whining, resisting; 2 = Screaming; 3 = Screaming, hitting, other aggression

BEHAVIOR – Behavior Likert Scale

Behavior Observation Form

Name: _____ **Date(s):** _____ **Staff:** _____ **Date:** _____

Antecedents	Behavior	Consequence
Start Time:		
End Time:		
Intensity Level:		
Setting:		
Initials of Staff:		
Activity: _____		

Antecedents	Behavior	Consequence
Start Time:		
End Time:		
Intensity Level:		
Setting:		
Initials of Staff:		
Activity: _____		

Antecedents	Behavior	Consequence
Start Time:		
End Time:		
Intensity Level:		
Setting:		
Initials of Staff:		
Activity: _____		

Record level for each behavior: 1 = mild, 2 = moderate, 3 = severe

Level 1 - Mild Protest	Level 2 - Moderate Protest	Level 3 - Severe Protest
Repetitive requests	Tossing or spreading materials	Physical assaults on adults
Task avoidance	Making more demanding requests	Physical assaults on peers
Facial gracing/frown	Hard tapping on surfaces	Running from class/building
Attempting to make physical contact	Being out of seat	Throwing heavy objects
Putting head down	Engaging in self-injurious behavior	

Show Me the Data! By Leon-Guerrero, Matsumoto, & Martin © 2011. AAPC. www.aapcpublishing.net
BEHAVIOR – Behavior Observation Form

Staff:	Date:

Behavioral Program

Child:	Date(s):

Describe the behavior in a measurable way: _____

_____

_____

_____

When is the behavior most likely to occur? _____

What currently occurs immediately before and after the behavior?

Before: _____

After: _____

Describe any modifications to the environment that will be made in an attempt to prevent the behavior from occurring:

_____

_____

_____

When the behavior does occur, what will be the response of the staff and/or the consequence for the child?

_____

_____

_____

_____

This plan will be reviewed on:_____

Duration Recording

Name:		Staff:		Date:

Behavior:		Date(s):	

Occurrence	Date	Time of Behavior		Total Time
		Start	End	
Example	5/5/10	10:05	10:15	10 min
1				
2				
3				
4				
5				
6				
7				
8				
9				
10				

Frequency Data

Name: _____

Behavior: _____

Date(s): _____

Staff: _____

Date: _____

Initials	Activity	Frequency	Total	Comments
Example Initials of observer		|||| ||||	10	Listening to music/no instruments today

Scatterplot – Sample

Sudent Name: Paul   **Staff:**   **Date:**

Behavior: Pinching adults

Note: This sheet is often used to collect data on challenging behaviors that have been targeted for behavior change.

Legend:
- 0 times (empty box)
- 1-2 times (diagonal line)
- 3-4 times (X)
- 5+ times (filled black box)

Time	Date	Date	Date	Date	Date	Date	Date	Date	Date	Date	Date	Date	Date
8:00													
8:15	■												
8:30			/	■	/	/	/	■					
9:00			/		X	X	X						
9:15													
9:30													
10:00													
10:15													
10:30													
11:00													
11:15			/	■	X	X	X	■					
11:30			■		X	X	X						
12:00				X									
12:15													
12:30													
1:00													
1:15													
1:30													
2:00													
2:15													
2:30													
3:00													
3:15													
3:30													

Comments:

Mark a line in the box corresponding to the number of occurrences of the target behavior.

Show Me the Data! By Leon-Guerrero, Matsumoto, & Martin © 2011. AAPC. www.aapcpublishing.net
BEHAVIOR – Scatterplot – Sample

Scatterplot

Student Name: _____ **Staff:** _____ **Date:** _____

Behavior: _____

Note: This sheet is often used to collect data on challenging behaviors that have been targeted for behavior change.

| ☐ 0 times | ◨ 1-2 times | ⊠ 3-4 times | ■ 5+ times |

Time	Date	Date	Date	Date	Date	Date	Date	Date	Date	Date	Date	Date	Date	Date	Date
8:00															
8:15															
8:30															
9:00															
9:15															
9:30															
10:00															
10:15															
10:30															
11:00															
11:15															
11:30															
12:00															
12:15															
12:30															
1:00															
1:15															
1:30															
2:00															
2:15															
2:30															
3:00															
3:15															
3:30															

Comments:

Mark a line in the box corresponding to the number of occurrences of the target behavior.

Show Me the Data! By Leon-Guerrero, Matsumoto, & Martin © 2011. AAPC. www.aapcpublishing.net
BEHAVIOR – Scatterplot

CHECK-OFF CHARTS

Data Check-Off Chart

Staff: _____ Date: _____

To be posted in the classroom, on a clipboard, or kept in a data notebook.

Child's Name:	Date:	Date:	Date:	Date:	Date:	Date:	Date:	Date:
• Cooperative activity	Y N P	Y N P	Y N P	Y N P	Y N P	Y N P	Y N P	Y N P
• End/begin activity	Y N P	Y N P	Y N P	Y N P	Y N P	Y N P	Y N P	Y N P
• Initiate peer interactions	Y N P	Y N P	Y N P	Y N P	Y N P	Y N P	Y N P	Y N P
• Multistep directions	Y N P	Y N P	Y N P	Y N P	Y N P	Y N P	Y N P	Y N P
• Problem solving	Y N P	Y N P	Y N P	Y N P	Y N P	Y N P	Y N P	Y N P
• Verbal sequences	Y N P	Y N P	Y N P	Y N P	Y N P	Y N P	Y N P	Y N P
Child's Name:	Date:	Date:	Date:	Date:	Date:	Date:	Date:	Date:
• Play cooperatively	Y N P	Y N P	Y N P	Y N P	Y N P	Y N P	Y N P	Y N P
• Use pronouns	Y N P	Y N P	Y N P	Y N P	Y N P	Y N P	Y N P	Y N P
• Contingent statements	Y N P	Y N P	Y N P	Y N P	Y N P	Y N P	Y N P	Y N P
• Why questions	Y N P	Y N P	Y N P	Y N P	Y N P	Y N P	Y N P	Y N P
• Coat on/off	Y N P	Y N P	Y N P	Y N P	Y N P	Y N P	Y N P	Y N P
Child's Name:	Date:	Date:	Date:	Date:	Date:	Date:	Date:	Date:
• Blend sounds	Y N P	Y N P	Y N P	Y N P	Y N P	Y N P	Y N P	Y N P
• Claim/defend possessions	Y N P	Y N P	Y N P	Y N P	Y N P	Y N P	Y N P	Y N P
• Complete transitions	Y N P	Y N P	Y N P	Y N P	Y N P	Y N P	Y N P	Y N P
• Complete toileting routine	Y N P	Y N P	Y N P	Y N P	Y N P	Y N P	Y N P	Y N P
• Phonetic sounds	Y N P	Y N P	Y N P	Y N P	Y N P	Y N P	Y N P	Y N P
• Quantitative concepts	Y N P	Y N P	Y N P	Y N P	Y N P	Y N P	Y N P	Y N P
• Turn taking	Y N P	Y N P	Y N P	Y N P	Y N P	Y N P	Y N P	Y N P

Circle response using key.

Key:

Y = Yes   N = No   P = Prompt

Staff Check-Off Chart

	Staff:											
	Date:											

To be posted in the clipboard, or kept in a data notebook.

Name of Staff Responsible:	Date:	Date:	Date:	Date:	Date:	Date:	Date:	Date:	Date:	Date:	Date:	Date:
Child's Name:												
Child's Name:												
Child's Name:												
Child's Name:												
Child's Name:												
Staff Name:	Date:	Date:	Date:	Date:	Date:	Date:	Date:	Date:	Date:	Date:	Date:	Date:
Child's Name:												
Child's Name:												
Child's Name:												
Child's Name:												
Child's Name:												
Staff Name:	Date:	Date:	Date:	Date:	Date:	Date:	Date:	Date:	Date:	Date:	Date:	Date:
Child's Name:												
Child's Name:												
Child's Name:												
Child's Name:												

Note. Staff checks or initials box corresponding to the child when data on IEP objectives have been taken.

Show Me the Data! By Leon-Guerrero, Matsumoto, & Martin © 2011. AAPC. www.aapcpublishing.net
CHECK-OFF CHARTS – Staff Check-Off Chart

COGNITIVE

Basic Shapes

Staff: **Date:**

Name:

Objective:

Criteria:

Date:

	■	●	◀	▮	Other:
Expressive					
Receptive					

Date:

	■	●	◀	▮	Other:
Expressive					
Receptive					

Date:

	■	●	◀	▮	Other:
Expressive					
Receptive					

Date:

	■	●	◀	▮	Other:
Expressive					
Receptive					

Date:

	■	●	◀	▮	Other:
Expressive					
Receptive					

Date:

	■	●	◀	▮	Other:
Expressive					
Receptive					

Key:

Expressive: Can student answer a shape question verbally?

Receptive: Can student follow direction involving a shape or point to shape?

Use a +/- score

Basic Shapes

Name: _____ **Staff:** _____ **Date:** _____

Objective: _____

Criteria: _____

Date:						
Expressive						
Receptive						

Date:						
Expressive						
Receptive						

Date:						
Expressive						
Receptive						

Date:						
Expressive						
Receptive						

Date:						
Expressive						
Receptive						

Date:						
Expressive						
Receptive						

Key:

Expressive: Can student answer a shape question verbally?

Receptive: Can student follow direction involving a shape or point to shape?

Use a +/– score

Show Me the Data! By Leon-Guerrero, Matsumoto, & Martin © 2011. AAPC. www.aapcpublishing.net
COGNITIVE – Basic Shapes

Blending Sounds

Name: _____ Staff: _____ Date: _____

Objective: _____ Criteria: _____

Date	Word(s)/Sound(s) Given	Child Response			Comment
		I	G/V	R	
		I	G/V	R	
		I	G/V	R	
		I	G/V	R	
		I	G/V	R	
		I	G/V	R	
		I	G/V	R	
		I	G/V	R	
		I	G/V	R	
		I	G/V	R	
		I	G/V	R	
		I	G/V	R	
		I	G/V	R	
		I	G/V	R	
		I	G/V	R	
		I	G/V	R	
		I	G/V	R	
		I	G/V	R	

Circle response using key.

Key:

I = Independent   G/V = Gestural/Verbal   R = Refusal

Show Me the Data! By Leon-Guerrero, Matsumoto, & Martin © 2011. AAPC. www.aapcpublishing.net
COGNITIVE – Blending Sounds

Body Parts

Staff:	Date:

Name:	
Objective:	Criteria:

Date	
Head	
Tummy	
Nose	
Shoulders	
Ears	
Thumb	
Neck	
Chest	

Date	
Head	
Tummy	
Nose	
Shoulders	
Ears	
Thumb	
Neck	
Chest	

Date	
Head	
Tummy	
Nose	
Shoulders	
Ears	
Thumb	
Neck	
Chest	

Date	
Head	
Tummy	
Nose	
Shoulders	
Ears	
Thumb	
Neck	
Chest	

Date	
Head	
Tummy	
Nose	
Shoulders	
Ears	
Thumb	
Neck	
Chest	

Date	
Head	
Tummy	
Nose	
Shoulders	
Ears	
Thumb	
Neck	
Chest	

Record responses using key.

Key:

+ = Correct Response   − = Incorrect Response /No Response   P = Prompted

Show Me the Data! By Leon-Guerrero, Matsumoto, & Martin © 2011. AAPC. www.aapcpublishing.net
COGNITIVE – Body Parts

Choice Making

Staff:	Date:

Name:

Objective:	Criteria:

Date:

Object Presented	Object Student Chose	Refusal
1. _____ 2. _____ 3. _____		Yes/No

Date:

Object Presented	Object Student Chose	Refusal
1. _____ 2. _____ 3. _____		Yes/No

Date:

Object Presented	Object Student Chose	Refusal
1. _____ 2. _____ 3. _____		Yes/No

Date:

Object Presented	Object Student Chose	Refusal
1. _____ 2. _____ 3. _____		Yes/No

Date:

Object Presented	Object Student Chose	Refusal
1. _____ 2. _____ 3. _____		Yes/No

Date:

Object Presented	Object Student Chose	Refusal
1. _____ 2. _____ 3. _____		Yes/No

Score by circling Yes/No.

Show Me the Data! By Leon-Guerrero, Matsumoto, & Martin © 2011. AAPC. www.aapcpublishing.net
COGNITIVE – Choice Making

Colors

Staff:	Date:

Name:	
Objective:	Criteria:

Trial #	1	2	3	4	5	6	7	8	9	10
Red										
Blue										
Yellow										
Green										
Orange										
Brown										
Black										
Purple										
Pink										
White										

Trial #	1	2	3	4	5	6	7	8	9	10
Red										
Blue										
Yellow										
Green										
Orange										
Brown										
Black										
Purple										
Pink										
White										

Record responses using key.

Key:

+ = Correct   − = Incorrect   P = Prompt

Completing Activities

Name:

Objective:

Criteria:

Staff:

Date:

Date	Activity	Prompts	Date	Activity	Prompts	Date	Activity	Prompts
		I G/V PP FP R			I G/V PP FP R			I G/V PP FP R
		I G/V PP FP R			I G/V PP FP R			I G/V PP FP R
		I G/V PP FP R			I G/V PP FP R			I G/V PP FP R
		I G/V PP FP R			I G/V PP FP R			I G/V PP FP R
		I G/V PP FP R			I G/V PP FP R			I G/V PP FP R
		I G/V PP FP R			I G/V PP FP R			I G/V PP FP R
		I G/V PP FP R			I G/V PP FP R			I G/V PP FP R
		I G/V PP FP R			I G/V PP FP R			I G/V PP FP R
		I G/V PP FP R			I G/V PP FP R			I G/V PP FP R
		I G/V PP FP R			I G/V PP FP R			I G/V PP FP R
		I G/V PP FP R			I G/V PP FP R			I G/V PP FP R
		I G/V PP FP R			I G/V PP FP R			I G/V PP FP R
		I G/V PP FP R			I G/V PP FP R			I G/V PP FP R
		I G/V PP FP R			I G/V PP FP R			I G/V PP FP R
		I G/V PP FP R			I G/V PP FP R			I G/V PP FP R

Circle responses using key.

Key:

I = Independent

G/V = Gestural/Verbal

PP = Partial Physical Assistance

FP = Full Partial Assistance

R = Refusal

Completing Multistep Task

Name: _____   **Staff:** _____   **Date:** _____

Objective: _____

Criteria: _____

Date	Task	Step 1	Step 2	Step 3	Step 4	Step 5
	Familiar Task:					
	Student Performance:	I G/V PP FP R	I G/V PP FP R	I G/V PP FP R	I G/V PP FP R	I G/V PP FP R

Date	Task	Step 1	Step 2	Step 3	Step 4	Step 5
	Familiar Task:					
	Student Performance:	I G/V PP FP R	I G/V PP FP R	I G/V PP FP R	I G/V PP FP R	I G/V PP FP R

Date	Task	Step 1	Step 2	Step 3	Step 4	Step 5
	Familiar Task:					
	Student Performance:	I G/V PP FP R	I G/V PP FP R	I G/V PP FP R	I G/V PP FP R	I G/V PP FP R

Date	Task	Step 1	Step 2	Step 3	Step 4	Step 5
	Familiar Task:					
	Student Performance:	I G/V PP FP R	I G/V PP FP R	I G/V PP FP R	I G/V PP FP R	I G/V PP FP R

Circle responses using key.

Key:

I = Independent

G/V = Gestural/Verbal

PP = Partial Physical Assistance

FP = Full Partial Assistance

R = Refusal

Show Me the Data! By Leon-Guerrero, Matsumoto, & Martin © 2011. AAPC. www.aapcpublishing.net
COGNITIVE – Completing Multistep Task

Concepts

Staff:	Date:

Name:

Objective: | **Criteria:**

Size		Quality		Quantity		Spatial		Temporal	
Big		Hot		All		In		Yesterday	
Tall		Cold		More		Out		Today	
Little		Wet		Empty		Under		Tomorrow	
Thick		Dry		Many		Bottom		Early	
Thin		Same		Few		To		Later	
Fat		Different		Lots		Here		Last	
Small		Slow		None		Beside		Before	
Short		Fast		Each		Next to		After	
Large		Good		Some		Back		First	
Skinny		Bad		Full		Middle		If-then	
Tiny		Rough		Less		Down			
Gigantic		Smooth		Any		Between			
Chubby		Light				Front			
Long		Heavy				Last			
		Loud				Up			
		Quiet				There			
		Hard				Behind			
		Soft				In back of			
		Sweet				In front of			
		Sour				First			

Record response using key.

Key:

+ = Correct

− = Incorrect

NR = No Response

Show Me the Data! By Leon-Guerrero, Matsumoto, & Martin © 2011. AAPC. www.aapcpublishing.net
COGNITIVE – Concepts

Counting 1-10

Staff:	Date:

Name:		
Objective:	Criteria:	

Date:	1	2	3	4	5	6	7	8	9	10
Student Response										

Date:	1	2	3	4	5	6	7	8	9	10
Student Response										

Date:	1	2	3	4	5	6	7	8	9	10
Student Response										

Date:	1	2	3	4	5	6	7	8	9	10
Student Response										

Date:	1	2	3	4	5	6	7	8	9	10
Student Response										

Date:	1	2	3	4	5	6	7	8	9	10
Student Response										

Date:	1	2	3	4	5	6	7	8	9	10
Student Response										

Date:	1	2	3	4	5	6	7	8	9	10
Student Response										

Date:	1	2	3	4	5	6	7	8	9	10
Student Response										

Record response using key.

Key:

+ = Correct

− = Incorrect/No Response

P = Prompt

Show Me the Data! By Leon-Guerrero, Matsumoto, & Martin © 2011. AAPC. www.aapcpublishing.net
COGNITIVE – Counting 1-10

Letters of the Alphabet – Recognition

Staff: | **Date:**

Name:

Objective:

Criteria:

Letters	Date:	Date:	Date:	Date:	Date:	Date:	Date:	Date:	Date:	Date:	Date:	Date:	Date:	Date:	Date:	Date:	Date:	Date:	Date:	Date:	Date:	Date:	Date:	Date:	Date:	Date:
A																										
B																										
C																										
D																										
E																										
F																										
G																										
H																										
I																										
J																										
K																										
L																										
M																										
N																										
O																										
P																										
Q																										
R																										
S																										
T																										
U																										
V																										
W																										
X																										
Y																										
Z																										

Record response using key.

Key:

+ = Correct Response

– = Incorrect Response/ No Response

P = Prompted

Letters of the Alphabet – Sounds

Staff:	Date:

Name:
Objective:
Criteria:

Sounds	Date:	Date:	Date:	Date:	Date:	Date:	Date:	Date:	Date:	Date:	Date:	Date:	Date:	Date:	Date:	Date:	Date:	Date:	Date:	Date:	Date:	Date:	Date:	Date:	Date:	Date:	Date:
A																											
B																											
C																											
D																											
E																											
F																											
G																											
H																											
I																											
J																											
K																											
L																											
M																											
N																											
O																											
P																											
Q																											
R																											
S																											
T																											
U																											
V																											
W																											
X																											
Y																											
Z																											

Record response using key.

Key:
+ = Correct Response
− = Incorrect Response/ No Response
P = Prompted

Matching

Staff:				**Date:**	

Name:

Objective: | **Criteria:**

Date	Object	Student Response	Object	Student Response.	Comments
		I G/V PP FP R		I G/V PP FP R	
		I G/V PP FP R		I G/V PP FP R	
		I G/V PP FP R		I G/V PP FP R	
		I G/V PP FP R		I G/V PP FP R	
		I G/V PP FP R		I G/V PP FP R	
		I G/V PP FP R		I G/V PP FP R	
		I G/V PP FP R		I G/V PP FP R	
		I G/V PP FP R		I G/V PP FP R	
		I G/V PP FP R		I G/V PP FP R	
		I G/V PP FP R		I G/V PP FP R	
		I G/V PP FP R		I G/V PP FP R	
		I G/V PP FP R		I G/V PP FP R	
		I G/V PP FP R		I G/V PP FP R	
		I G/V PP FP R		I G/V PP FP R	
		I G/V PP FP R		I G/V PP FP R	
		I G/V PP FP R		I G/V PP FP R	
		I G/V PP FP R		I G/V PP FP R	
		I G/V PP FP R		I G/V PP FP R	
		I G/V PP FP R		I G/V PP FP R	
		I G/V PP FP R		I G/V PP FP R	
		I G/V PP FP R		I G/V PP FP R	
		I G/V PP FP R		I G/V PP FP R	
		I G/V PP FP R		I G/V PP FP R	
		I G/V PP FP R		I G/V PP FP R	
		I G/V PP FP R		I G/V PP FP R	
		I G/V PP FP R		I G/V PP FP R	
		I G/V PP FP R		I G/V PP FP R	
		I G/V PP FP R		I G/V PP FP R	

Circle responses using key.

Key:

I = Independent

G/V = Gestural/Verbal

PP = Partial Physical

FP = Full Physical

R = Refusal

COGNITIVE – Matching

Sequencing Story

Staff:	Date:

Name:	
Objective:	Criteria:

Date	Story	Part 1	Part 2	Part 3	Part 4	Part 5
	Given by Teacher					
	Recounted by Student					

Date	Story	Part 1	Part 2	Part 3	Part 4	Part 5
	Given by Teacher					
	Recounted by Student					

Date	Story	Part 1	Part 2	Part 3	Part 4	Part 5
	Given by Teacher					
	Recounted by Student					

Date	Story	Part 1	Part 2	Part 3	Part 4	Part 5
	Given by Teacher					
	Recounted by Student					

Date	Story	Part 1	Part 2	Part 3	Part 4	Part 5
	Given by Teacher					
	Recounted by Student					

Date	Story	Part 1	Part 2	Part 3	Part 4	Part 5
	Given by Teacher					
	Recounted by Student					

Record response (given by teacher/recounted by student) using checkmarks.

Staff:	Date:

Name:

Objective:

Criteria:

Sounds First Set	Date	Date	Date	Date	Date	Date	Date	Date	Date	Date	Date	Date	Date	Date	Date	Date	Date	Date	Date	Date
a																				
m																				
s																				
e																				
r																				
d																				
f																				
i																				
th																				
t																				
n																				
c																				
o																				
h																				
u																				
g																				
l																				
w																				
sh																				

Record response using key.

Key:

+ = Correct Response   – = Incorrect Response/No Response   P = Prompted

Staff:	Date:

Name:
Objective:
Criteria:

Sounds Second Set	Date	Date	Date	Date	Date	Date	Date	Date	Date	Date	Date	Date	Date	Date	Date	Date	Date	Date	Date	Date
l																				
k																				
o																				
v																				
p																				
ch																				
e																				
b																				
ing																				
i																				
y																				
er																				
x																				
oo																				
j																				
y																				
wh																				
qu																				
z																				
u																				

Record response using key.

Key:

+ = Correct Response   − = Incorrect Response/No Response   P = Prompted

Show Me the Data! By Leon-Guerrero, Matsumoto, & Martin © 2011. AAPC. www.aapcpublishing.net

COGNITIVE – Sound-Symbol Correspondence

Specific Directions

Staff:		**Date:**	

Name:

Objective: | **Criteria:**

Date:

Trial	1	2	3	4	5	6	7	8	9	10
Come here										
Sit down										
Stand up										
Stop										
Clap hands										
Stomp feet										
Watch me										

Date:

Trial	1	2	3	4	5	6	7	8	9	10
Come here										
Sit down										
Stand up										
Stop										
Clap hands										
Stomp feet										
Watch me										

Date:

Trial	1	2	3	4	5	6	7	8	9	10
Come here										
Sit down										
Stand up										
Stop										
Clap hands										
Stomp feet										
Watch me										

Record response using key.
Key:
+ = Correct Response
– = Incorrect Response/No Response
P = Prompted

Show Me the Data! By Leon-Guerrero, Matsumoto, & Martin © 2011. AAPC. www.aapcpublishing.net
COGNITIVE – Specific Directions

COMMUNICATION

Articulation

Name: _____ **Staff:** _____ **Date:** _____

Objective: _____ **Criteria:** _____

Date	Word Modeled	What Child Said	Comments

Use Comments column to note any prompting necessary.

Asking/Answering Questions

Staff: **Date:**

Name:

Objective: **Criteria:**

Date	Question Asked (Adult/Peer/Child)	Child's Response	Comments

Use Comments column to note any prompting necessary.

Show Me the Data! By Leon-Guerrero, Matsumoto, & Martin © 2011. AAPC. www.aapcpublishing.net
COMMUNICATION – Asking/Answering Questions

Communicative Exchanges

Staff:	Date:

Name:

Objective:	**Criteria:**

Date	Engagement	Request/ Comment	Response	Correspondence	Communicative Partner	Comments
	Y N P	Y N P	Y N P	Y N P	Y N P	
	Y N P	Y N P	Y N P	Y N P	Y N P	
	Y N P	Y N P	Y N P	Y N P	Y N P	
	Y N P	Y N P	Y N P	Y N P	Y N P	
	Y N P	Y N P	Y N. P	Y N P	Y N P	
	Y N P	Y N P	Y N P	Y N P	Y N P	
	Y N P	Y N P	Y N P	Y N P	Y N P	
	Y N P	Y N P	Y N P	Y N P	Y N P	
	Y N P	Y N P	Y N P	Y N P	Y N P	
	Y N P	Y N P	Y N P	Y N P	Y N P	
	Y N P	Y N P	Y N P	Y N P	Y N P	
	Y N P	Y N P	Y N P	Y N P	Y N P	
	Y N P	Y N P	Y N P	Y N P	Y N P	
	Y N P	Y N P	Y N P	Y N P	Y N P	
	Y N P	Y N P	Y N P	Y N P	Y N P	
	Y N P	Y N P	Y N P	Y N P	Y N P	
	Y N P	Y N P	Y N P	Y N P	Y N P	
	Y N P	Y N P	Y N P	Y N P	Y N P	
	Y N P	Y N P	Y N P	Y N P	Y N P	
	Y N P	Y N P	Y N P	Y N P	Y N P	
	Y N P	Y N P	Y N P	Y N P	Y N P	
	Y N P	Y N P	Y N P	Y N P	Y N P	
	Y N P	Y N P	Y N P	Y N P	Y N P	
	Y N P	Y N P	Y N P	Y N P	Y N P	
	Y N P	Y N P	Y N P	Y N P	Y N P	
	Y N P	Y N P	Y N P	Y N P	Y N P	

Circle response using key.

Key:

Y = Yes

N = No

P = Prompt

Engagement: Does student have partner's attention?
Request/Comment: Did student make a request or comment?
Response: Did partner respond? Was partner aware of request?
Correspondence: Did student get what he wanted?

Show Me the Data! By Leon-Guerrero, Matsumoto, & Martin © 2011. AAPC. www.aapcpublishing.net
COMMUNICATION – Communicative Exchanges

| Communicative Initiations | | | Staff: | Date: |

Name:			
Objective:		Criteria:	

Date	Initiation, Greeting, or Statement by Child	Who Was the Communicative Partner?	Comments

Use Comments column to note any prompting necessary.

Ending Conversations

Name:

Objective: **Criteria:**

Date	Ending Conversation Statement Said by Child (e.g., good-bye)	Child Waits Until End of Conversation to Leave	Child Uses Communicative Partner's Name	Comments

Use Comments column to note any prompting necessary.

Expressive Vocabulary

	Staff:	Date:

Name:

Objective: | **Criteria:**

Record expressive vocabulary used by the student.

Date:	Date:	Date:
1.	1.	1.
2.	2.	2.
3.	3.	3.
4.	4.	4.
5.	5.	5.
6.	6.	6.
7.	7.	7.
8.	8.	8.
9.	9.	9.
10.	10.	10.

Date:	Date:	Date:
1.	1.	1.
2.	2.	2.
3.	3.	3.
4.	4.	4.
5.	5.	5.
6.	6.	6.
7.	7.	7.
8.	8.	8.
9.	9.	9.
10.	10.	10.

Date:	Date:	Date:
1.	1.	1.
2.	2.	2.
3.	3.	3.
4.	4.	4.
5.	5.	5.
6.	6.	6.
7.	7.	7.
8.	8.	8.
9.	9.	9.
10.	10.	10.

Show Me the Data! By Leon-Guerrero, Matsumoto, & Martin © 2011. AAPC. www.aapcpublishing.net

Expressive Word List

| Staff: | Date: |

Name:

Objective: | **Criteria:**

Expressive Words																
Date:																
Date:																
Date:																
Date:																
Date:																
Date:																
Date:																
Date:																
Date:																
Date:																
Date:																
Date:																

KEY:

To the right of the date, record + or – based on student performance.

Show Me the Data! By Leon-Guerrero, Matsumoto, & Martin © 2011. AAPC. www.aapcpublishing.net
COMMUNICATION – Expressive Word List

Gain Partner's Attention

Staff:	Date:

Name:	
Objective:	**Criteria:**

Date	Did Child Gain Partner's Attention?	If Yes, How? *(Say name, tap shoulder, etc.)*	Child Used Partner's Name Correctly?	Comments
	Yes / No		Yes / No	
	Yes / No		Yes / No	
	Yes / No		Yes / No	
	Yes / No		Yes / No	
	Yes / No		Yes / No	
	Yes / No		Yes / No	
	Yes / No		Yes / No	
	Yes / No		Yes / No	
	Yes / No		Yes / No	
	Yes / No		Yes / No	
	Yes / No		Yes / No	
	Yes / No		Yes / No	
	Yes / No		Yes / No	
	Yes / No		Yes / No	
	Yes / No		Yes / No	
	Yes / No		Yes / No	
	Yes / No		Yes / No	

Circle yes/no to record responses.

Use Comments column to note any prompting necessary.

Show Me the Data! By Leon-Guerrero, Matsumoto, & Martin © 2011. AAPC. www.aapcpublishing.net

Identifying Familiar People

Name: _____ **Staff:** _____ **Date:** _____

Objective: _____

Criteria: _____

Familiar Person	Date	Trial 1	Trial 2	Trial 3	Trial 4	Trial 5	Trial 6	Trial 7	Trial 8	Trial 9	Trial 10

Familiar Person	Date	Trial 1	Trial 2	Trial 3	Trial 4	Trial 5	Trial 6	Trial 7	Trial 8	Trial 9	Trial 10

Familiar Person	Date	Trial 1	Trial 2	Trial 3	Trial 4	Trial 5	Trial 6	Trial 7	Trial 8	Trial 9	Trial 10

Record response using key.

Key:

+ = Correct

– = Incorrect/No Response

P = Prompt

COMMUNICATION – Identifying Familiar People

Oral-Motor Imitation

Staff:	Date:

Name:	
Objective:	Criteria:

Date:

Trial	1	2	3	4	5	6	7	8	9	10
Open										
Close										
Blow										

Date:

Trial	1	2	3	4	5	6	7	8	9	10
Open										
Close										
Blow										

Date:

Trial	1	2	3	4	5	6	7	8	9	10
Open										
Close										
Blow										

Date:

Trial	1	2	3	4	5	6	7	8	9	10
Open										
Close										
Blow										

Record response using key.

Key:

+ = Correct

− = Incorrect/No Response

P = Prompt

Receptive Word List

Staff:	Date:

Name:

Objective: | **Criteria:**

Receptive Words														
Date:														
Date:														
Date:														
Date:														
Date:														
Date:														
Date:														
Date:														
Date:														
Date:														
Date:														
Date:														

Record response using key.

Key:

+ = Correct Response

– = Incorrect Response

Show Me the Data! By Leon-Guerrero, Matsumoto, & Martin © 2011. AAPC. www.aapcpublishing.net
COMMUNICATION – Receptive Word List

Reciprocal Response

Name:

Staff:

Date:

Objective:

Criteria:

Date	Question Asked (by Adult or Peer)	Child's Response	Question Asked (by Child to Reciprocate)	Comments
10/22/08	"What is your name?"	"Robert"	"What is your name?"	Independent

Respond to Name

| Staff: | Date: |

Name:

| Objective: | Criteria: |

Date	Response to Name	Comments
	N L V B O	
	N L V B O	
	N L V B O	
	N L V B O	
	N L V B O	
	N L V B O	
	N L V B O	
	N L V B O	
	N L V B O	
	N L V B O	
	N L V B O	
	N L V B O	
	N L V B O	

Circle responses using key.

Key:

N = No Response
L = Looks at Speaker
V = Verbal Response
B = Both Looks and Verbalizes
O = Other (must specify)

Show Me the Data! By Leon-Guerrero, Matsumoto, & Martin © 2011. AAPC. www.aapcpublishing.net
COMMUNICATION – Respond to Name

GENERAL

5 Trial

Name: Staff:

Objective: Criteria: Date:

Trial	Comments		Trial	Comments
5			5	
4			4	
3			3	
2			2	
1			1	

Trial	Comments		Trial	Comments
5			5	
4			4	
3			3	
2			2	
1			1	

Trial	Comments		Trial	Comments
5			5	
4			4	
3			3	
2			2	
1			1	

Trial	Comments		Trial	Comments
5			5	
4			4	
3			3	
2			2	
1			1	

Activity Matrix – Sample

To Be Posted in the Classroom

Student Names	A.M.	Z.S.	P.V.	E.W.	O.W.
Arrival/Dismissal	• Initiate peer interactions	• Respond with contingent statements • Put coat on and off	• Give full name and age		• Understand increase speech intelligibility • Understand 4- to 5-word phrases • Follow 2-step novel direction
Snack/Lunch	• Solve problems • Initiate peer interactions			• Answer/ask "wh" questions • Gain partner's attention	• Increase speech intelligibility • Understand 4- to 5-word phrases
Circle	• Join in cooperative activity • Perform verbal sequences	• Respond with contingent statements	• Produce age-appropriate sounds	• Answer/ask "wh" questions • Follow group directions • Tailor sit	• Follow 2-step novel direction
Reading	• Perform verbal sequences	• Correctly use pronouns • Respond with contingent statements	• Copy/trace letters of name • Do rhyming sounds	• Increase mandibular (lower jaw) excursion • Perform sound-syllable correspondence	• Increase speech intelligibility
Math	• Demonstrate emerging tripod grasp for shapes	• Use a tripod grasp to write name	• Match #s to sets of 1-10	• Demonstrate understanding of quantitative concepts	• Complete activity • Increase speech intelligibility
Small Group/ Journal	• Solve problems • Demonstrate emerging tripod grasp for shapes	• Correctly use pronouns • Respond to "why" questions	• Produce age-appropriate sounds	• Answer/ask "wh" questions • Gain partner's attention.	• Increase speech intelligibility • Understand 4- to 5-word phrases
Free Choice	• Initiate peer interactions • Manipulate small objects • Follow directions • Join in cooperative activity	• Play cooperatively • Respond with contingent statements	• Initiate cooperative activity • Name gender of self and others • State birthday	• Answer/ask "wh" questions • Claim/defend possessions • Gain partner's attention	• Engage with peer in play • Increase speech intelligibility • Understand 4- to 5-word phrases
Playcourt/Gym	• Solve problems • Initiate peer interactions	• Play cooperatively		• Maintain balance on one foot	
Transition	• Solve problems • Follow directions	• Put coat on and off		• Complete transitions	• Follow 2-step novel direction
Toileting				• Complete toileting routine independently	

Activity Matrix

Daily Activities	Child:	Child:	Child:	Child:	Staff:	Date:

Activity Matrix for a Preschool/Kindergarten Classroom

Staff: Date:

Activity	Child:	Child:	Child:	Child:
Arrival/Circle				
Center Time				
Small Group				
Outside Play				
Snack				

Activity Matrix for a Play Date

Staff: _____   Date: _____

Activity	Child:	Child:	Child:	Child:
Arrival				
Structured Play				
Free Time (Highly Preferred Activities)				
Outside Play				
Snack				

Show Me the Data! By Leon-Guerrero, Matsumoto, & Martin © 2011. AAPC. www.aapcpublishing.net
GENERAL – Activity Matrix for a Play Date

Activity Matrix for a Social Skills Group

Activity	Child:	Child:	Child:	Child:
Arrival/Meeting				
Small Group/ Dyad				
Large Group				
Snack				
Closing Meeting				

Staff: _____ Date: _____

Show Me the Data! By Leon-Guerrero, Matsumoto, & Martin © 2011. AAPC. www.aapcpublishing.net
GENERAL – Activity Matrix for a Social Skills Group

Anecdotal Record

	Staff:	Date:

Name:

Objective:	Criteria:

Date	Incident	Comment

Basic Prompting 0-4

	Staff:	Date:

Name:		
Objective:	Criteria:	

	4 3 2 1 0	4 3 2 1 0	4 3 2 1 0	4 3 2 1 0	4 3 2 1 0	4 3 2 1 0
Date:						
Activity:						

	4 3 2 1 0	4 3 2 1 0	4 3 2 1 0	4 3 2 1 0	4 3 2 1 0	4 3 2 1 0
Date:						
Activity:						

	4 3 2 1 0	4 3 2 1 0	4 3 2 1 0	4 3 2 1 0	4 3 2 1 0	4 3 2 1 0
Date:						
Activity:						

	4 3 2 1 0	4 3 2 1 0	4 3 2 1 0	4 3 2 1 0	4 3 2 1 0	4 3 2 1 0
Date:						
Activity:						

Record response using key.

Key:
4 = Independent
3 = Gestural/Verbal
2 = Partial Physical
1 = Full Physical
0 = Resistance/Refusal

Daily Data Sheet – Sample

Staff:	Date:

Child: Robert   **Dates:** 10/08

Program: Gross Imitation

Controlling Prompt:

Stimulus	Child's Response	EC
Clap Hands	+	
	+	
Stamd up	PP	
	+	
Stomp feet	FP	
	PP	
Tap Head	+	
	+	
Touch nose	+	
	PP	

Program: Drawing Imitation

Controlling Prompt:

Stimulus	Child's Response	EC
Square	FP	
	FP	
Triangle	FP	
	PP	
+	+	
	PP	
/	+	
	+	
\	+	
	+	

Program: Gross Imitation

Controlling Prompt:

Stimulus	Child's Response	EC
Give food	PP	
	PP	
	+	
	−	X
	PP	
Say "hi"	PP	
	+	
	−	X
	PP	
	PP	

Program: Color Identification

Controlling Prompt:

Stimulus	Child's Response	EC
Red	PP	
	+	
Blue	G	
	G	
Green	PP	
	+	
Yellow	PP	
	PP	
Brown	FP	
	FP	

Program: Requesting

Controlling Prompt:

Stimulus	Child's Response	EC
"See and Say"	+	
	+	
Elmo Toy	+	
	+	
Bubbles	PP	
	+	
Stickers	−	X
	PP	
Dot art	PP	
	+	

Program: Label Actions in Pictures

Controlling Prompt:

Stimulus	Child's Response	EC
Jumping	PP	
	PP	
Running	G	
	+	
Swimming	FP	
	G	
Writing	G	
	+	
Sleeping	+	
	+	

Program: Appropriate Play – Farm

Controlling Prompt:

Stimulus	Child's Response	EC
Drive tractor	PP	
	G	
Feed animal	G	
	+	
Put animals in barn	G	
	PP	
Ride horse	+	
	+	
Walk animal	G	
	+	

Program: Gross Imitation

Controlling Prompt:

Stimulus	Child's Response	EC
Flowers	FP	
	Pp	
Strawberries	G	
	PP	
Spider	−	X
	PP	
Shoe	+	
	+	
Hat	+	
	PP	

Program: Gross Imitation

Controlling Prompt:

Stimulus	Child's Response	EC
Line up	+	
	+	
Get coat	−	X
	PP	
Wash hands	PP	
	PP	
Sit down	G	
	+	
Stand up	G	
	+	

Record response using the key.

Key:
P = Prompt
G = Gesture

FP = Full Prompt
PP = Partial Prompt

+ = Independent Correct
− = Incorrect

NOTE: EC refers to Error Correction. This column should be marked if the trial included an error correction.

Show Me the Data! By Leon-Guerrero, Matsumoto, & Martin © 2011. AAPC. www.aapcpublishing.net
GENERAL – Daily Data Sheet – Sample

Daily Data Sheet

Staff:	Date:

Child:	Dates:

Program:

Controlling Prompt:

Stimulus	Child's Response	EC

Program:

Controlling Prompt:

Stimulus	Child's Response	EC

Program:

Controlling Prompt:

Stimulus	Child's Response	EC

Program:

Controlling Prompt:

Stimulus	Child's Response	EC

Program:

Controlling Prompt:

Stimulus	Child's Response	EC

Program:

Controlling Prompt:

Stimulus	Child's Response	EC

Program:

Controlling Prompt:

Stimulus	Child's Response	EC

Program:

Controlling Prompt:

Stimulus	Child's Response	EC

Program:

Controlling Prompt:

Stimulus	Child's Response	EC

Record response using the key.

Key:
P = Prompt
G = Gesture

FP = Full Prompt
PP = Partial Prompt

+ = Independent Correct
- = Incorrect

NOTE: EC refers to Error Correction. This column should be marked if the trial included an error correction.

Show Me the Data! By Leon-Guerrero, Matsumoto, & Martin © 2011. AAPC. www.aapcpublishing.net
GENERAL – Daily Data Sheet

Data by Activity – Multiple Students (1) – Sample

| Activity: | Dramatic Play | | Week of: | June 2-6, 2010 | Staff: | Jones | Date: 6/2–6/6/10 |

Record response using key.

Key: + = Correct – = Incorrect

Ilene

Goal 1: Give play ideas to peers (play leaders).				
Trials:	+	+	–	–	+

Goal 2: Use kind problem-solving strategies in play				
Trials:	+	–	–	+	

| Goal 3: | | | | |
| Trials: | | | | |

| Goal 4: | | | | |
| Trials: | | | | |

Susan

Goal 1: Respond to a peer's request in play.			
Trials:	–	–	–	

Goal 2: Use 2 words together.			
Trials:	+	+	+	+

| Goal 3: | | | |
| Trials: | | | |

| Goal 4: | | | |
| Trials: | | | |

Student 3

| Goal 1: |
| Trials: |
| Goal 2: |
| Trials: |
| Goal 3: |
| Trials: |
| Goal 4: |
| Trials: |

Student 4

| Goal 1: |
| Trials: |
| Goal 2: |
| Trials: |
| Goal 3: |
| Trials: |
| Goal 4: |
| Trials: |

Student 5

| Goal 1: |
| Trials: |
| Goal 2: |
| Trials: |
| Goal 3: |
| Trials: |
| Goal 4: |
| Trials: |

Student 6

| Goal 1: |
| Trials: |
| Goal 2: |
| Trials: |
| Goal 3: |
| Trials: |
| Goal 4: |
| Trials: |

Student 7

| Goal 1: |
| Trials: |
| Goal 2: |
| Trials: |
| Goal 3: |
| Trials: |
| Goal 4: |
| Trials: |

Student 8

| Goal 1: |
| Trials: |
| Goal 2: |
| Trials: |
| Goal 3: |
| Trials: |
| Goal 4: |
| Trials: |

Student 9

| Goal 1: |
| Trials: |
| Goal 2: |
| Trials: |
| Goal 3: |
| Trials: |
| Goal 4: |
| Trials: |

Student 10

| Goal 1: |
| Trials: |
| Goal 2: |
| Trials: |
| Goal 3: |
| Trials: |
| Goal 4: |
| Trials: |

Data by Activity – Multiple Students (1)

| Activity: | | Week of: | | Staff: | | Date: | |

Student 1		Student 2		Student 3		Student 4		Student 5	
Goal 1:		Goal 1:		Goal 1:		Goal 1:		Goal 1:	
Trials:		Trials:		Trials:		Trials:		Trials:	
Goal 2:		Goal 2:		Goal 2:		Goal 2:		Goal 2:	
Trials:		Trials:		Trials:		Trials:		Trials:	
Goal 3:		Goal 3:		Goal 3:		Goal 3:		Goal 3:	
Trials:		Trials:		Trials:		Trials:		Trials:	
Goal 4:		Goal 4:		Goal 4:		Goal 4:		Goal 4:	
Trials:		Trials:		Trials:		Trials:		Trials:	

Student 6		Student 7		Student 8		Student 9		Student 10	
Goal 1:		Goal 1:		Goal 1:		Goal 1:		Goal 1:	
Trials:		Trials:		Trials:		Trials:		Trials:	
Goal 2:		Goal 2:		Goal 2:		Goal 2:		Goal 2:	
Trials:		Trials:		Trials:		Trials:		Trials:	
Goal 3:		Goal 3:		Goal 3:		Goal 3:		Goal 3:	
Trials:		Trials:		Trials:		Trials:		Trials:	
Goal 4:		Goal 4:		Goal 4:		Goal 4:		Goal 4:	
Trials:		Trials:		Trials:		Trials:		Trials:	

Record response using key.
Key: + = Correct — = Incorrect

Show Me the Data! *Show Me the Data!* By Leon-Guerrero, Matsumoto, & Martin © 2011. AAPC. www.aapcpublishing.net
GENERAL – Data by Activity – Multiple Students (1)

Data by Activity – Multiple Students (2) – Sample

Staff: McBride   **Date:** 6/12/10

Date:

Activity: Circle Data Sheet

M.B.
Does he talk about something that happened in the past?
Criteria: ≥ 3 events per week
Prompt: visual cues provided if necessary

Y / N	Y / N	Y / N

M.F.
Does he produce a variety of vowel sounds and vowel tracks?
Criteria: 80% accuracy per week for two weeks

Y / N	Y / N	Y / N

Does he make eye contact with the person he is talking/signing to?
Criteria: 5 times weekly for each of three weeks

Y / N	Y / N	Y / N

C.W.
Does he use two words together when he talks?
Criteria: ≥5 examples of targeted utterance types per week for 2 weeks
Write words you hear:

S.H.
Does she independently raise her hand to make a choice?
Criteria: Once a day on 4/5 days across two weeks

Mon	Tue	Wed	Thu	Fri
Y / N	Y / N	Y / N	Y / N	Y / N

M.O.
Does he name objects in pictures?
Criteria: ≥4 times/week across two weeks
List objects:
1.
2.
3.
4.
5.

C.P.
Does she count up to 5 objects?
Criteria: 4/5 opportunities in one week, across two weeks

Y / N

M.S.
Does she identify an item (show me ___) when shown two or more items?
Criteria: ≥5 times/week for two weeks

Y / N	Y / N	Y / N

C.A.

A.J.
Does he calm down when frustrated with a difficult task using different strategies?
Criteria: 5 naturally occurring opportunities

	M	T	W	Th	F
Opp	Y / N	Y / N	Y / N	Y / N	Y / N
Calm Down?	Y / N	Y / N	Y / N	Y / N	Y / N

J.B.
Does he stay with the group and raise his hand to make a choice?
Criteria: 4/5 days in one week, across two weeks

Stay with Group

M	T	Wed	Th	F
Y / N	Y / N	Y / N	Y / N	Y / N

Raise Hand

M	T	Wed	Th	F
Y / N	Y / N	Y / N	Y / N	Y / N

Record response circling X (yes) or N (no).

Data by Activity – Multiple Students (2)

| Date: | | Activity: | | Staff: | | Date: |

Student 1

Objective:

Criteria:

Prompt:

Y / N	Y / N	Y / N

Data collection method (individualized per student's objects/criteria/prompt)

Student 2

Objective:

Criteria:

Prompt:

Y / N	Y / N	Y / N

Data collection method (individualized per student's objects/criteria/prompt)

Student 3

Objective:

Criteria:

Prompt:

Y / N	Y / N	Y / N

Data collection method (individualized per student's objects/criteria/prompt)

Student 4

Objective:

Criteria:

Prompt:

Y / N	Y / N	Y / N

Data collection method (individualized per student's objects/criteria/prompt)

Student 5

Objective:

Criteria:

Prompt:

Y / N	Y / N	Y / N

Data collection method (individualized per student's objects/criteria/prompt)

Student 6

Objective:

Criteria:

Prompt:

Y / N	Y / N	Y / N

Data collection method (individualized per student's objects/criteria/prompt)

Student 7

Objective:

Criteria:

Prompt:

Y / N	Y / N	Y / N

Data collection method (individualized per student's objects/criteria/prompt)

Student 8

Objective:

Criteria:

Prompt:

Y / N	Y / N	Y / N

Data collection method (individualized per student's objects/criteria/prompt)

Student 9

Objective:

Criteria:

Prompt:

Y / N	Y / N	Y / N

Data collection method (individualized per student's objects/criteria/prompt)

Student 10

Objective:

Criteria:

Prompt:

Y / N	Y / N	Y / N

Data collection method (individualized per student's objects/criteria/prompt)

Record response circling Y (yes) or N (no).

Show Me the Data! By Leon-Guerrero, Matsumoto, & Martin © 2011. AAPC. www.aapcpublishing.net
GENERAL – Data by Activity – Multiple Students (2)

Data by Number Amount

Staff:	Date:

Name:

Objective 1:	Criteria:

Date

Frequency										
20	20	20	20	20	20	20	20	20	20
19	19	19	19	19	19	19	19	19	19
18	18	18	18	18	18	18	18	18	18
17	17	17	17	17	17	17	17	17	17
16	16	16	16	16	16	16	16	16	16
15	15	15	15	15	15	15	15	15	15
14	14	14	14	14	14	14	14	14	14
13	13	13	13	13	13	13	13	13	13
12	12	12	12	12	12	12	12	12	12
11	11	11	11	11	11	11	11	11	11
10	10	10	10	10	10	10	10	10	10
9	9	9	9	9	9	9	9	9	9
8	8	8	8	8	8	8	8	8	8
7	7	7	7	7	7	7	7	7	7
6	6	6	6	6	6	6	6	6	6
5	5	5	5	5	5	5	5	5	5
4	4	4	4	4	4	4	4	4	4
3	3	3	3	3	3	3	3	3	3
2	2	2	2	2	2	2	2	2	2
1	1	1	1	1	1	1	1	1	1
0	0	0	0	0	0	0	0	0	0

Name:

Objective 2:	Criteria:

Date

Frequency										
20	20	20	20	20	20	20	20	20	20
19	19	19	19	19	19	19	19	19	19
18	18	18	18	18	18	18	18	18	18
17	17	17	17	17	17	17	17	17	17
16	16	16	16	16	16	16	16	16	16
15	15	15	15	15	15	15	15	15	15
14	14	14	14	14	14	14	14	14	14
13	13	13	13	13	13	13	13	13	13
12	12	12	12	12	12	12	12	12	12
11	11	11	11	11	11	11	11	11	11
10	10	10	10	10	10	10	10	10	10
9	9	9	9	9	9	9	9	9	9
8	8	8	8	8	8	8	8	8	8
7	7	7	7	7	7	7	7	7	7
6	6	6	6	6	6	6	6	6	6
5	5	5	5	5	5	5	5	5	5
4	4	4	4	4	4	4	4	4	4
3	3	3	3	3	3	3	3	3	3
2	2	2	2	2	2	2	2	2	2
1	1	1	1	1	1	1	1	1	1
0	0	0	0	0	0	0	0	0	0

Please circle appropriate number.

Show Me the Data! By Leon-Guerrero, Matsumoto, & Martin © 2011. AAPC. www.aapcpublishing.net
GENERAL – Data by Number Amount

	Staff:	Date:

Data by Student – Multiple Objectives – Sample

Name: John	**Week of:** 12/9/10

OBJECTIVE	Free Choice	Snack	Outside/Gym	Circle	Arrival/ Departure	Criteria	Met
Continue to play (i.e., sustain engagement)	+ blocks 2 minutes					1 activity 1 min 3 session	
Imitate actions with objects	+/– (G/PP) Hammer and Bash-A-Ball			+/– (FP) clapper ("Happy & You Know It …")		3 actions 3 session	
Respond to peers	+/– (PP) Sara gave John a car in block area		+/– (VP) accepted marker from Billy			2 peers 2contexts	
1-step directions w/ cues				+/– (PP) "Clean up"		3 direct. 3 session	
Wash hands		– Refused				4 out of 4	
Try new foods		– Refused to try muffin				3 foods 3 session	
Total Comm. To request			+/– (V) "b" sound for ball			10 examples	
Look toward object while adult points				+ good-bye song (bird)		3 objects 3 session	

Record response using key.

KEY:
+ = Independently
+/- = W/ prompt/assistance (specify)
- = Refusal
NO = No Opportunity

PROMPTS
FP = Full Physical
PP = Partial Physical
V = Verbal
G = Gestural

EXAMPLES
Verbal Imitation + "bye"
Motor Imitation +/- (PP) Clapping
Stacking - blocks

Staff:	Date:

Data by Student – Multiple Objectives

Name:	Week of:

OBJECTIVE	Activity 1	Activity 2	Activity 3	Activity 4	Activity 5	Activity 6	Criteria	Met

Record response using key.

KEY:
+ = Independently
+/- = W/ prompt/assistance (specify)
- = Refusal
NO = No Opportunity

PROMPTS
FP = Full Physical
PP = Partial Physical
V = Verbal
G = Gestural

EXAMPLES
Verbal Imitation + "bye"
Motor Imitation +/- (PP) Clapping
Stacking - blocks

Free-Choice Data Matrix – Sample

Week of: | **Staff:** Wilkerson | **Date:** 5/20/10

Student	Objective	What Adult Can Say/Do	Prompting Level	Record Data/Comments/Initials	Criteria
	1. Independently engage in board games with rules for the duration of game.	Get game, have Jose identify a peer to play with. Say "let's play."	I		2/2 for 3 wks
	2. Independently self-regulate when upset by asking for help, identifying affect, or selecting a problem solving strategy.	Use picture symbols to show Jose what he needs to do (ex: symbol of "calm body" or "get backpack").	G		2/3 for 3 wks
Jose	3. Independently verbally initiate with peers in structured and unstructured settings.		V, M		4x ea. setting/ wk for 3 wks
	4. Follow a 2-part non-routine direction.	Give directions with two actions or two description words.	V		3/4 for 2 wks
	5. Comment on his or others' behavior.		V, M	Write utterances	3/4 over 2 days
	1. Independently follow 2-step routine classroom directions. Must respond within 5 seconds.	Give a clear 2-step direction and use current prompting level to ensure follow-through.	G	"hang up coat and backpack"; "clean up & sit down at circle"; "clean up & line up"; "line up & wash hands"; "get coat and backpack".	9/10 over 2 days w/ 5 dif dir.
	2. Independently engage in imaginary play schemes with peers lasting 4+ minutes.	Use current prompting level to engage Sally in imaginary play with peers.	M		3 diff schemes 2 ea. over 2 wks
Sally	3. Engage in games with rules.	Wait for her turn, follow sequence, and appropriately begin and end (to game completion).	V		3 age app. social, 3 board
	5. Independently maintain her play when peers join to play with the same items.		V		4/5 for 2 wks.
	6. Use 2 words or signs.	Use verbal/sign models and expansion techniques.	M	Write utterances	2/3 w/ 3 dif. act. over 2 days
	7. Will verbally initiate and respond to peer.	Use peer-mediated interaction strategies.		Initiate | respond	1x / day
	1. Ind. use simple strategies to resolve conflict with peers.	Prompt Jackson to walk away, report to an adult, make demands.	I		4/5 for 2 wks.
Jackson	2. When asked to share by a peer, independently share or exchange objects/toys with that peer.	Set up situations to encourage sharing, such as limiting materials or using favorite toys.	I		4/5 for 2 wks.
	3. Independently join others in cooperative play.	Help Jackson to use verbal and non-verbal strategies to enter play.	I		5x for 2 wks.
	4. Verbally respond on topic to peer in naturalistic setting.		V	Write utterances	4/5 over 2 dys.

Record response using key.

Key:
I = Independent
G = Gestural
V = Verbal
PP = Partial Physical
FP = Full Physical
R = Resistance/Refusal
M = Model

Show Me the Data! By Leon-Guerrero, Matsumoto, & Martin © 2011, AAPC. www.aapcpublishing.net
GENERAL – Free-Choice Data Matrix – Sample

Free-Choice Data Matrix

Week of:			Staff:			Date:	

Student	Objective	What Adult Can Say/Do	Prompting Level	Record Data/Comments/Initials	Criteria

Record reponse using key.

Key:

I = Independent	V = Verbal	FP = Full Physical	M = Model
G = Gestural	PP = Partial Physical	R = Resistance/Refusal	

Interval Recording – Sample

Staff:		**Date:**

Name: Kelsey	**Date:** March 16	
Interval: 10 seconds	**Activity:** Morning Circle	
	Condition: Intervention (student wears gloves)	

Interval	Behavior ___ ___	Engaged (+/–)	Interval	Behavior ___ ___	Engaged (+/–)	Interval	Behavior ___ ___	Engaged (+/–)
1	+	–	36	–	+	71		
2	+	–	37	–	+	72		
3	–	+	38	–	+	73		
4	–	+	39	–	+	74		
5	–	+	40	–	+	75		
6	+	–	41	–	–	76		
7	–	+	42	–	+	77		
8	–	+	43	–	+	78		
9	–	+	44	–	+	79		
10	+	–	45	–	+	80		
11	–	+	46	+	+	81		
12	–	+	47	–	+	82		
13	–	+	48	–	+	83		
14	–	+	49	–	+	84		
15	–	–	50	–	+	85		
16	+	–	51	–	+	86		
17	–	–	52	–	+	87		
18	–	+	53	–	+	88		
19	–	+	54	–	+	89		
20	–	+	55	–	+	90		
21	–	+	56	–	+	91		
22	–	+	57	–	–	92		
23	+	+	58	–	+	93		
24	–	+	59	+	–	94		
25	–	+	60	+	–	95		
26	–	+	61	+	+	96		
27	–	+	62	+	–	97		
28	–	–	63	+	–	98		
29	–	+	64	–	+	99		
30	–	–	65	–	+	100		
31	–	+	66			**Total +**	14	49
32	–	+	67			**Total intervals**	65	65
33	+	+	68			**Divide for %**	21% of time picking hands	75% of time engaged
34	–	+	69					
35	+	–	70					

Key:

At the end of 10 seconds, record "+" if the behavior is occurring; record "–" if the behavior is not occurring.

Show Me the Data! By Leon-Guerrero, Matsumoto, & Martin © 2011. AAPC. www.aapcpublishing.net
GENERAL – Interval Recording – Sample

Interval Recording

Staff:	Date:

Name:	Date:
Interval:	Activity:
	Condition:

Interval	Behavior _____ _____	Engaged (+/−)	Interval	Behavior _____ _____	Engaged (+/−)	Interval	Behavior _____ _____	Engaged (+/−)
1			36			71		
2			37			72		
3			38			73		
4			39			74		
5			40			75		
6			41			76		
7			42			77		
8			43			78		
9			44			79		
10			45			80		
11			46			81		
12			47			82		
13			48			83		
14			49			84		
15			50			85		
16			51			86		
17			52			87		
18			53			88		
19			54			89		
20			55			90		
21			56			91		
22			57			92		
23			58			93		
24			59			94		
25			60			95		
26			61			96		
27			62			97		
28			63			98		
29			64			99		
30			65			100		
31			66					
32			67			Total +		
33			68			Total intervals		
34			69			Divide for %		
35			70					

Key:

At the end of 10 seconds, record "+" if the behavior is occurring; record "−" if the behavior is not occurring.

Show Me the Data! By Leon-Guerrero, Matsumoto, & Martin © 2011. AAPC. www.aapcpublishing.net
GENERAL – Interval Recording

Likert Scale – Sample

Staff: James	**Date:** 6/18/10

Student: Elizabeth

Objective: Responds to greetings by peers																		
Almost Always (5+)				X	X	X												
Sometimes (3-4)																		
Almost Never (1-3)			X															
Never (0)	X	X																
Date:	1/5	1/12	1/19	1/26	2/2	2/9												

Objective: Takes turns during social games																		
Almost Always (5+)																		
Sometimes (3-4)				X		X												
Almost Never (1-3)	X		X															
Never (0)		X																
Date:	1/5	1/12	1/19	1/26	2/2	2/9												

Objective: Accepts changes in the routine																		
Almost Always (5+)				X														
Sometimes (3-4)					X													
Almost Never (1-3)	X	X		X														
Never (0)			X															
Date:	1/5	1/12	1/19	1/26	2/2	2/9												

Key:

Mark an "x" in the box according to the number of times the behavior occurs. This will give a visual display of the data.

Almost Always: The behavior occurs 5 or more times.
Sometimes: The behavior occurs 3-4 times.
Almost Never: The behavior never 1-3 times.
Never: The behavior occurs 0 times.

Show Me the Data! By Leon-Guerrero, Matsumoto, & Martin © 2011. AAPC. www.aapcpublishing.net
GENERAL – Likert Scale – Sample

Likert Scale

	Staff:	Date:

Student:

Objective:																				
Almost Always (5+)																				
Sometimes (3-4)																				
Almost Never (1-3)																				
Never (0)																				
Date																				

Objective:																				
Almost Always (5+)																				
Sometimes (3-4)																				
Almost Never (1-3)																				
Never (0)																				
Date																				

Objective:																				
Almost Always (5+)																				
Sometimes (3-4)																				
Almost Never (1-3)																				
Never (0)																				
Date																				

Objective:																				
Almost Always (5+)																				
Sometimes (3-4)																				
Almost Never (1-3)																				
Never (0)																				
Date																				

Key:
Mark an "x" in the box according to the number of times the behavior occurs. This will give a visual display of the data.

Almost Always: The behavior occurs 5 or more times.
Sometimes: The behavior occurs 3-4 times.
Almost Never: The behavior never 1-3 times.
Never: The behavior occurs 0 times.

| | | | Mass Trials | | | | Staff: | | | Date: | |

<table>
<tr><td colspan="3">Mass Trials</td><td>Staff:</td><td>Date:</td></tr>
</table>

Mass Trials Staff: Date:

Name:

Objective: **Criteria:**

Date	Level of Prompt	Trials										Total
		1	2	3	4	5	6	7	8	9	10	/
		1	2	3	4	5	6	7	8	9	10	/
		1	2	3	4	5	6	7	8	9	10	/
		1	2	3	4	5	6	7	8	9	10	/
		1	2	3	4	5	6	7	8	9	10	/
		1	2	3	4	5	6	7	8	9	10	/
		1	2	3	4	5	6	7	8	9	10	/
		1	2	3	4	5	6	7	8	9	10	/
		1	2	3	4	5	6	7	8	9	10	/
		1	2	3	4	5	6	7	8	9	10	/
		1	2	3	4	5	6	7	8	9	10	/
		1	2	3	4	5	6	7	8	9	10	/
		1	2	3	4	5	6	7	8	9	10	/
		1	2	3	4	5	6	7	8	9	10	/
		1	2	3	4	5	6	7	8	9	10	/
		1	2	3	4	5	6	7	8	9	10	/
		1	2	3	4	5	6	7	8	9	10	/
		1	2	3	4	5	6	7	8	9	10	/
		1	2	3	4	5	6	7	8	9	10	/
		1	2	3	4	5	6	7	8	9	10	/
		1	2	3	4	5	6	7	8	9	10	/
		1	2	3	4	5	6	7	8	9	10	/

Key:

Circle correct trials. Mark with an "X" incorrect trials.

Show Me the Data! By Leon-Guerrero, Matsumoto, & Martin © 2011. AAPC. www.aapcpublishing.net
GENERAL – Mass Trials

Outcome or Objective Update

Staff:	Date:

Name:	School Year:

Goal Area: ☐ Adaptive   ☐ Cognitive   ☐ Social   ☐ Communication   ☐ Fine/Gross Motor

Objective:

Date:	Date:	Date:

Status		Status		Status	
☐ Continue	☐ Discontinue	☐ Continue	☐ Discontinue	☐ Continue	☐ Discontinue
☐ Modify	☐ Close	☐ Modify	☐ Close	☐ Modify	☐ Close

Objective:

Date:	Date:	Date:

Status		Status		Status	
☐ Continue	☐ Discontinue	☐ Continue	☐ Discontinue	☐ Continue	☐ Discontinue
☐ Modify	☐ Close	☐ Modify	☐ Close	☐ Modify	☐ Close

Objective:

Date:	Date:	Date:

Status		Status		Status	
☐ Continue	☐ Discontinue	☐ Continue	☐ Discontinue	☐ Continue	☐ Discontinue
☐ Modify	☐ Close	☐ Modify	☐ Close	☐ Modify	☐ Close

Check the appropriate boxes.

Show Me the Data! By Leon-Guerrero, Matsumoto, & Martin © 2011. AAPC. www.aapcpublishing.net
GENERAL – Outcome or Objective Update

Repeated Trials – Sample

Staff: Ramirez **Date:** 5/10/10

Name: Diego

School Year: 2010-2011

Skill Area: Cognitive

Objective Numbers: Visual Performance – Matching

Test Date:	2/3	2/4	2/7	2/11	2/13	2/14														
Objective:	(10)	X10	(10)	(10)	(10)	10	10	10	10	10	10	10	10	10	10	10	10	10	10	10
Match picture to picture	X9	(9)	X9	X9	(9)	9	9	9	9	9	9	9	9	9	9	9	9	9	9	9
	X8	(8)	(8)	(8)	X8	8	8	8	8	8	8	8	8	8	8	8	8	8	8	8
	(7)	X7	(7)	X7	(7)	7	7	7	7	7	7	7	7	7	7	7	7	7	7	7
	(6)	(6)	6	(6)	X6	6	6	6	6	6	6	6	6	6	6	6	6	6	6	6
	X5	(5)	(5)	(5)	(5)	5	5	5	5	5	5	5	5	5	5	5	5	5	5	5
	(4)	X4	(4)	X4	(4)	4	4	4	4	4	4	4	4	4	4	4	4	4	4	4
	(3)	(3)	3	(3)	(3)	3	3	3	3	3	3	3	3	3	3	3	3	3	3	3
	X2	(2)	(2)	(2)	X2	2	2	2	2	2	2	2	2	2	2	2	2	2	2	2
	X1	X1	(1)	X1	(1)	1	1	1	1	1	1	1	1	1	1	1	1	1	1	1
	0	0	0	0	0	0	0	0	0	0	0	0	0	0	0	0	0	0	0	0

Initiated: ____ Terminated: ____ # Days in Progress: ____

Test Date:																				
Objective:	10	10	10	10	10	10	10	10	10	10	10	10	10	10	10	10	10	10	10	10
	9	9	9	9	9	9	9	9	9	9	9	9	9	9	9	9	9	9	9	9
	8	8	8	8	8	8	8	8	8	8	8	8	8	8	8	8	8	8	8	8
	7	7	7	7	7	7	7	7	7	7	7	7	7	7	7	7	7	7	7	7
	6	6	6	6	6	6	6	6	6	6	6	6	6	6	6	6	6	6	6	6
	5	5	5	5	5	5	5	5	5	5	5	5	5	5	5	5	5	5	5	5
	4	4	4	4	4	4	4	4	4	4	4	4	4	4	4	4	4	4	4	4
	3	3	3	3	3	3	3	3	3	3	3	3	3	3	3	3	3	3	3	3
	2	2	2	2	2	2	2	2	2	2	2	2	2	2	2	2	2	2	2	2
	1	1	1	1	1	1	1	1	1	1	1	1	1	1	1	1	1	1	1	1
	0	0	0	0	0	0	0	0	0	0	0	0	0	0	0	0	0	0	0	0

Initiated: ____ Terminated: ____ # Days in Progress: ____

Test Date:																				
Objective:	10	10	10	10	10	10	10	10	10	10	10	10	10	10	10	10	10	10	10	10
	9	9	9	9	9	9	9	9	9	9	9	9	9	9	9	9	9	9	9	9
	8	8	8	8	8	8	8	8	8	8	8	8	8	8	8	8	8	8	8	8
	7	7	7	7	7	7	7	7	7	7	7	7	7	7	7	7	7	7	7	7
	6	6	6	6	6	6	6	6	6	6	6	6	6	6	6	6	6	6	6	6
	5	5	5	5	5	5	5	5	5	5	5	5	5	5	5	5	5	5	5	5
	4	4	4	4	4	4	4	4	4	4	4	4	4	4	4	4	4	4	4	4
	3	3	3	3	3	3	3	3	3	3	3	3	3	3	3	3	3	3	3	3
	2	2	2	2	2	2	2	2	2	2	2	2	2	2	2	2	2	2	2	2
	1	1	1	1	1	1	1	1	1	1	1	1	1	1	1	1	1	1	1	1
	0	0	0	0	0	0	0	0	0	0	0	0	0	0	0	0	0	0	0	0

Initiated: ____ Terminated: ____ # Days in Progress: ____

Circle correct responses. "X" incorrect responses.

Show Me the Data! By Leon-Guerrero, Matsumoto, & Martin © 2011. AAPC. www.aapcpublishing.net

GENERAL – Repeated Trials – Sample

Repeated Trials

Staff:	Date:

Name:

School Year:

Skill Area:

Objective Numbers:

Test Date:

Objective:

10	10	10	10	10	10	10	10	10	10	10	10	10	10	10	10	10	10	10
9	9	9	9	9	9	9	9	9	9	9	9	9	9	9	9	9	9	9
8	8	8	8	8	8	8	8	8	8	8	8	8	8	8	8	8	8	8
7	7	7	7	7	7	7	7	7	7	7	7	7	7	7	7	7	7	7
6	6	6	6	6	6	6	6	6	6	6	6	6	6	6	6	6	6	6
5	5	5	5	5	5	5	5	5	5	5	5	5	5	5	5	5	5	5
4	4	4	4	4	4	4	4	4	4	4	4	4	4	4	4	4	4	4
3	3	3	3	3	3	3	3	3	3	3	3	3	3	3	3	3	3	3
2	2	2	2	2	2	2	2	2	2	2	2	2	2	2	2	2	2	2
1	1	1	1	1	1	1	1	1	1	1	1	1	1	1	1	1	1	1
0	0	0	0	0	0	0	0	0	0	0	0	0	0	0	0	0	0	0

Initiated: **Terminated:**   **# Days in Progress:**

Test Date:

Objective:

10	10	10	10	10	10	10	10	10	10	10	10	10	10	10	10	10	10	10
9	9	9	9	9	9	9	9	9	9	9	9	9	9	9	9	9	9	9
8	8	8	8	8	8	8	8	8	8	8	8	8	8	8	8	8	8	8
7	7	7	7	7	7	7	7	7	7	7	7	7	7	7	7	7	7	7
6	6	6	6	6	6	6	6	6	6	6	6	6	6	6	6	6	6	6
5	5	5	5	5	5	5	5	5	5	5	5	5	5	5	5	5	5	5
4	4	4	4	4	4	4	4	4	4	4	4	4	4	4	4	4	4	4
3	3	3	3	3	3	3	3	3	3	3	3	3	3	3	3	3	3	3
2	2	2	2	2	2	2	2	2	2	2	2	2	2	2	2	2	2	2
1	1	1	1	1	1	1	1	1	1	1	1	1	1	1	1	1	1	1
0	0	0	0	0	0	0	0	0	0	0	0	0	0	0	0	0	0	0

Initiated: **Terminated:**   **# Days in Progress:**

Test Date:

Objective:

10	10	10	10	10	10	10	10	10	10	10	10	10	10	10	10	10	10	10
9	9	9	9	9	9	9	9	9	9	9	9	9	9	9	9	9	9	9
8	8	8	8	8	8	8	8	8	8	8	8	8	8	8	8	8	8	8
7	7	7	7	7	7	7	7	7	7	7	7	7	7	7	7	7	7	7
6	6	6	6	6	6	6	6	6	6	6	6	6	6	6	6	6	6	6
5	5	5	5	5	5	5	5	5	5	5	5	5	5	5	5	5	5	5
4	4	4	4	4	4	4	4	4	4	4	4	4	4	4	4	4	4	4
3	3	3	3	3	3	3	3	3	3	3	3	3	3	3	3	3	3	3
2	2	2	2	2	2	2	2	2	2	2	2	2	2	2	2	2	2	2
1	1	1	1	1	1	1	1	1	1	1	1	1	1	1	1	1	1	1
0	0	0	0	0	0	0	0	0	0	0	0	0	0	0	0	0	0	0

Initiated: **Terminated:**   **# Days in Progress:**

Circle correct responses. "X" incorrect responses.

Show Me the Data! By Leon-Guerrero, Matsumoto, & Martin © 2011. AAPC. www.aapcpublishing.net
GENERAL – Repeated Trials – Sample

MOTOR

Balance Beam

	Staff:	Date:

Name:

Objective: | **Criteria:**

Date	Level of Support	Number of Steps Down	Comment
	1 2 3 4	0 1 2 >2	
	1 2 3 4	0 1 2 >2	
	1 2 3 4	0 1 2 >2	
	1 2 3 4	0 1 2 >2	
	1 2 3 4	0 1 2 >2	
	1 2 3 4	0 1 2 >2	
	1 2 3 4	0 1 2 >2	
	1 2 3 4	0 1 2 >2	
	1 2 3 4	0 1 2 >2	
	1 2 3 4	0 1 2 >2	
	1 2 3 4	0 1 2 >2	
	1 2 3 4	0 1 2 >2	
	1 2 3 4	0 1 2 >2	
	1 2 3 4	0 1 2 >2	
	1 2 3 4	0 1 2 >2	
	1 2 3 4	0 1 2 >2	
	1 2 3 4	0 1 2 >2	
	1 2 3 4	0 1 2 >2	

Circle level of support using key.

Key:

1 = One-Hand Support   3 = Verbal/Gestural

2 = Two-Hand Support   4 = Independent

Show Me the Data! By Leon-Guerrero, Matsumoto, & Martin © 2011. AAPC. www.aapcpublishing.net
MOTOR – Balance Beam

Copying

		Staff:	Date:

Name:

Objective:		Criteria:

		Trials					
Objective	**Date**	**1**	**2**	**3**	**4**	**5**	**Comments**
Copy Vertical Line		4 3 2 1	4 3 2 1	4 3 2 1	4 3 2 1	4 3 2 1	
Copy Horizontal Line		4 3 2 1	4 3 2 1	4 3 2 1	4 3 2 1	4 3 2 1	
Copy Circles		4 3 2 1	4 3 2 1	4 3 2 1	4 3 2 1	4 3 2 1	
Copy/Trace Name		4 3 2 1	4 3 2 1	4 3 2 1	4 3 2 1	4 3 2 1	

		Trials: Level of Assistance					
Objective	**Date**	**1**	**2**	**3**	**4**	**5**	**Comments**
Copy Vertical Line		4 3 2 1	4 3 2 1	4 3 2 1	4 3 2 1	4 3 2 1	
Copy Horizontal Line		4 3 2 1	4 3 2 1	4 3 2 1	4 3 2 1	4 3 2 1	
Copy Circles		4 3 2 1	4 3 2 1	4 3 2 1	4 3 2 1	4 3 2 1	
Copy/Trace Name		4 3 2 1	4 3 2 1	4 3 2 1	4 3 2 1	4 3 2 1	

Circle response using the key.

Key:

4 = Independent

3 = Verbal/Gestural

2 = Partial Physical

1 = Full Physical

0 = Refusal

Show Me the Data! By Leon-Guerrero, Matsumoto, & Martin © 2011. AAPC. www.aapcpublishing.net
MOTOR – Copying

General Motor Imitation

		Staff:	Date:

Name:

Objective: | **Criteria:**

Date	Action	Imitated +/-	Comments

Record response using key.

Key:

+ = Correct

− = Incorrect/No Response

P = Prompt

Show Me the Data! By Leon-Guerrero, Matsumoto, & Martin © 2011. AAPC. www.aapcpublishing.net
MOTOR – General Motor Imitation

Motor Skills 1

Name:

Staff:

Date:

Objective:

Criteria:

Date	Trial 1	Trial 2	Trial 3	Trial 4	Trial 5
Motor Skills					
	I G/V PP FP R	I G/V PP FP R	I G/V PP FP R	I G/V PP FP R	I G/V PP FP R
	I G/V PP FP R	I G/V PP FP R	I G/V PP FP R	I G/V PP FP R	I G/V PP FP R
	I G/V PP FP R	I G/V PP FP R	I G/V PP FP R	I G/V PP FP R	I G/V PP FP R

Date	Trial 1	Trial 2	Trial 3	Trial 4	Trial 5
Motor Skills					
	I G/V PP FP R	I G/V PP FP R	I G/V PP FP R	I G/V PP FP R	I G/V PP FP R
	I G/V PP FP R	I G/V PP FP R	I G/V PP FP R	I G/V PP FP R	I G/V PP FP R
	I G/V PP FP R	I G/V PP FP R	I G/V PP FP R	I G/V PP FP R	I G/V PP FP R

Circle responses using key.

Key:

I = Independent

G/V = Gestural/Verbal

PP = Partial Physical Assistance

FP = Full Partial Assistance

R = Refusal

Show Me the Data! By Leon-Guerrero, Matsumoto, & Martin © 2011. AAPC. www.aapcpublishing.net
MOTOR – Motor Skills 1

Motor Skills 2 – Sample

Staff: Smith **Date:** 10/23/10

Name:
Objective:	**Criteria:** N/A Multiple Skills

Trials: Level of Assistance							
Objective	**Date**	**1**	**2**	**3**	**4**	**5**	**Comments**
Kick Roling Ball	10/23	4	2	2	4	3	
Balance Beam	10/23	2	3	3	3	4	
Pedal Tricycle	10/25	2	4	4	2	4	
Steer Tricycle	10/25	3	3	2	3	4	

Trials: Level of Assistance							
Objective	**Date**	**1**	**2**	**3**	**4**	**5**	**Comments**
Trace simple shapes	10/22	3	3	4	3	3	
Copy simple shapes	10/22	2	3	3	2	3	
Cut on a straight line	10/22	4	4	4	4	4	
Cut a circle	10/22	3	3	2	2	2	

Record response using key.

Key:

4 = Independent   1 = Full Physical

3 = Verbal/Gestural   0 = Refusal

2 = Partial Physical

Motor Skills 2

Staff:	Date:

Name:

Objective:	Criteria:

				Trials: Level of Assistance			
Objective	Date	1	2	3	4	5	Comments

				Trials: Level of Assistance			
Objective	Date	1	2	3	4	5	Comments

Choose level of assistance using key.

Key:

4 = Independent   1 = Full Physical

3 = Verbal/Gestural   0 = Refusal

2 = Partial Physical

Show Me the Data! By Leon-Guerrero, Matsumoto, & Martin © 2011. AAPC. www.aapcpublishing.net
MOTOR – Motor Skills 2

Using Scissors

Name:

Objective: **Criteria:**

Date	Level of Assistance	Orientation	# of Snips	Comments
	4 3 2 1 0	+ −		
	4 3 2 1 0	+ −		
	4 3 2 1 0	+ −		
	4 3 2 1 0	+ −		
	4 3 2 1 0	+ −		
	4 3 2 1 0	+ −		
	4 3 2 1 0	+ −		
	4 3 2 1 0	+ −		
	4 3 2 1 0	+ −		
	4 3 2 1 0	+ −		
	4 3 2 1 0	+ −		
	4 3 2 1 0	+ −		
	4 3 2 1 0	+ −		
	4 3 2 1 0	+ −		
	4 3 2 1 0	+ −		
	4 3 2 1 0	+ −		
	4 3 2 1 0	+ −		

Circle response using key.

Key:

4 = Independent   1 = Full Physical   + = Correct

3 = Verbal/Gestural   0 = Refusal   − = Incorrect

2 = Partial Physical

Show Me the Data! By Leon-Guerrero, Matsumoto, & Martin © 2011. AAPC. www.aapcpublishing.net
MOTOR – Using Scissors

ROUTINES AND DIRECTIONS

Arrival/Dismissal Directions

Staff:	Date:

Name:

Objective:	Criteria:

Date	Arrival/Dismissal Directions	Level of Assistance
		I G/V PP FP R
		I G/V PP FP R
		I G/V PP FP R
		I G/V PP FP R
		I G/V PP FP R

Date	Arrival/Dismissal Directions	Level of Assistance
		I G/V PP FP R
		I G/V PP FP R
		I G/V PP FP R
		I G/V PP FP R
		I G/V PP FP R

Date	Arrival/Dismissal Directions	Level of Assistance
		I G/V PP FP R
		I G/V PP FP R
		I G/V PP FP R
		I G/V PP FP R
		I G/V PP FP R

Date	Arrival/Dismissal Directions	Level of Assistance
		I G/V PP FP R
		I G/V PP FP R
		I G/V PP FP R
		I G/V PP FP R
		I G/V PP FP R

Record response using key.

Key:
I = Independent
G/V = Gestural/Verbal
PP = Partial Physical
FP = Full Physical
R = Resistance/Refusal

Directive Commands

		Staff:	Date:

Name:	
Objective:	Criteria:

Example:

Direction	Trial 1	Trial 2	Trial 3	Trial 4	Trial 5	Trial 6	Trial 7	Trial 8	Trial 9	Trial 10
Line Up	+	+	+	+	P	P	–	P	+	+

Date:										
Direction	Trial 1	Trial 2	Trial 3	Trial 4	Trial 5	Trial 6	Trial 7	Trial 8	Trial 9	Trial 10

Date:										
Direction	Trial 1	Trial 2	Trial 3	Trial 4	Trial 5	Trial 6	Trial 7	Trial 8	Trial 9	Trial 10

Date:										
Direction	Trial 1	Trial 2	Trial 3	Trial 4	Trial 5	Trial 6	Trial 7	Trial 8	Trial 9	Trial 10

Circle response using key.

Key:
+ = Correct
– = Incorrect/No Response
P = Prompt

Show Me the Data! By Leon-Guerrero, Matsumoto, & Martin © 2011. AAPC. www.aapcpublishing.net
ROUTINES/DIRECTIONS – Directive Commands

Following Directions

	Staff:	Date:

Name:

Objective: | **Criteria:**

Date	Direction Given	Followed Direction?
		I G/V PP FP R
		I G/V PP FP R
		I G/V PP FP R
		I G/V PP FP R
		I G/V PP FP R
		I G/V PP FP R
		I G/V PP FP R
		I G/V PP FP R
		I G/V PP FP R
		I G/V PP FP R
		I G/V PP FP R
		I G/V PP FP R
		I G/V PP FP R
		I G/V PP FP R
		I G/V PP FP R
		I G/V PP FP R
		I G/V PP FP R
		I G/V PP FP R
		I G/V PP FP R
		I G/V PP FP R
		I G/V PP FP R
		I G/V PP FP R
		I G/V PP FP R

Circle response using key.

Key:

I = Independent   G/V = Gestural/Verbal Cue
PP = Partial Physical Assistance   FP = Full Physical Assistance
R = Resistance/Refusal

Response to Transition Cue

Staff:	Date:

Name:

Objective:	Criteria:

Date	Activity/Transition	Response to Cue
		I G/V PP FP R
		I G/V PP FP R
		I G/V PP FP R
		I G/V PP FP R
		I G/V PP FP R
		I G/V PP FP R
		I G/V PP FP R
		I G/V PP FP R
		I G/V PP FP R
		I G/V PP FP R
		I G/V PP FP R
		I G/V PP FP R
		I G/V PP FP R
		I G/V PP FP R
		I G/V PP FP R
		I G/V PP FP R
		I G/V PP FP R
		I G/V PP FP R
		I G/V PP FP R
		I G/V PP FP R
		I G/V PP FP R
		I G/V PP FP R
		I G/V PP FP R

Circle response using key.

Key:

I = Independent   G/V = Gestural/Verbal
PP = Partial Physical Assistance   FP = Full Physical Assistance
R = Refusal

Routine/Transitions

Staff: **Date:**

Name:

Objective: **Criteria:**

Date:

Activity	Level of Assistance				
	0	1	2	3	4
	0	1	2	3	4
	0	1	2	3	4
	0	1	2	3	4
	0	1	2	3	4
	0	1	2	3	4
	0	1	2	3	4
	0	1	2	3	4
	0	1	2	3	4
	0	1	2	3	4
	0	1	2	3	4
	0	1	2	3	4
	0	1	2	3	4
	0	1	2	3	4
	0	1	2	3	4

Date:

Activity	Level of Assistance				
	0	1	2	3	4
	0	1	2	3	4
	0	1	2	3	4
	0	1	2	3	4
	0	1	2	3	4
	0	1	2	3	4
	0	1	2	3	4
	0	1	2	3	4
	0	1	2	3	4
	0	1	2	3	4
	0	1	2	3	4
	0	1	2	3	4
	0	1	2	3	4
	0	1	2	3	4
	0	1	2	3	4

Date:

Activity	Level of Assistance				
	0	1	2	3	4
	0	1	2	3	4
	0	1	2	3	4
	0	1	2	3	4
	0	1	2	3	4
	0	1	2	3	4
	0	1	2	3	4
	0	1	2	3	4
	0	1	2	3	4
	0	1	2	3	4
	0	1	2	3	4
	0	1	2	3	4
	0	1	2	3	4
	0	1	2	3	4
	0	1	2	3	4

Date:

Activity	Level of Assistance				
	0	1	2	3	4
	0	1	2	3	4
	0	1	2	3	4
	0	1	2	3	4
	0	1	2	3	4
	0	1	2	3	4
	0	1	2	3	4
	0	1	2	3	4
	0	1	2	3	4
	0	1	2	3	4
	0	1	2	3	4
	0	1	2	3	4
	0	1	2	3	4
	0	1	2	3	4
	0	1	2	3	4

Circle level of assistance using key.

Key:
0 = Resistance/Refusal
1 = Full Physical
2 = Partial Physical
3 = Verbal/Gestural Prompt
4 = Independent

Show Me the Data! By Leon-Guerrero, Matsumoto, & Martin © 2011. AAPC. www.aapcpublishing.net
ROUTINES/DIRECTIONS – Routine/Transitions

Two-Step Directions

Name: _____ Staff: _____ Date: _____

Objective: _____ Criteria: _____

Date	Direction 1	Successful? Yes / No		Direction 2	Successful? Yes / No		Comment

SOCIAL

Accepting Items from Peers

Staff: **Date:**

Name:

Objective: **Criteria:**

Date	Item Offered by Peer/Adult (circle)	Level of Assistance (4,3,2,1,0)	Comments
	Peer Adult	4 3 2 1 0	
	Peer Adult	4 3 2 1 0	
	Peer Adult	4 3 2 1 0	
	Peer Adult	4 3 2 1 0	
	Peer Adult	4 3 2 1 0	
	Peer Adult	4 3 2 1 0	
	Peer Adult	4 3 2 1 0	
	Peer Adult	4 3 2 1 0	
	Peer Adult	4 3 2 1 0	
	Peer Adult	4 3 2 1 0	
	Peer Adult	4 3 2 1 0	

Circle level of assistance using key.

Key:
4 = Independent
3 = Verbal/Gestural
2 = Partial Physical
1 = Full Physical
0 = Refusal

Show Me the Data! By Leon-Guerrero, Matsumoto, & Martin © 2011. AAPC. www.aapcpublishing.net
SOCIAL – Accepting Items from Peers

Combined Data Collection and Matrix – Sample

Date: **Staff:** Hanson **Date:** 10/23/10

Skill Area	Child: Adam	Child: Kevin	Child: Miller	Child: Hannah	Notes:
Social	Program: Initiating — P + − +	Program: Initiating — P + + −	Program: Initiating — P P + +	Program: Initiating — + + + −	
	Program: Responding — P P + −	Program: Responding — + P + −	Program: Responding — + P + −	Program: Responding — − P + +	
Social	Program: Board Game (Turns Taken) — P + + +	Program: Board Game (Turns Taken) — P P + −	Program: Board Game (Turns Taken) — P + + +	Program: Board Game (Turns Taken) — P + + P	
Social	Program: Emotions (Label in Self and Others) — P + + −	Program: Emotions (Label in Self and others to include rationale) — P P + −	Program: Self Regulation (Use appropriate strategies to self-regulate) — + + + −	Program: Self Regulation (With adult assistance, will use appropriate strategies) — P + + −	

Record response using key.

Key:

+ = Independent/Correct   P = Prompted   – = No Response/Incorrect

Combined Data Collection and Matrix

Date: _____   Staff: _____   Date: _____

Date: _____

Skill Area	Child:	Child:	Child:	Notes:
	Program:	Program:	Program:	
	Program:	Program:	Program:	
	Program:	Program:	Program:	
	Program:	Program:	Program:	
	Program:	Program:	Program:	
	Program:	Program:	Program:	

Record response using key.

Key:

+ = Independent/Correct   P = Prompted   – = No Response/Incorrect   Y = Yes   N = N

Show Me the Data! By Leon-Guerrero, Matsumoto, & Martin © 2011. AAPC. www.aapcpublishing.net
SOCIAL – Combined Data Collection and Matrix

Cooperative Play

Staff: Jacobs   **Date:** 5/18/10

Name:

Objective:

Criteria:

Date	Play Activity	Prompting	Minutes Engaged in Play
	Ex. Barnyard Bingo	I G/V (PP) FP R	7
		I G/V PP FP R	
		I G/V PP FP R	
		I G/V PP FP R	
		I G/V PP FP R	
		I G/V PP FP R	
		I G/V PP FP R	
		I G/V PP FP R	
		I G/V PP FP R	
		I G/V PP FP R	
		I G/V PP FP R	
		I G/V PP FP R	

Date	Play Activity	Prompting	Minutes Engaged in Play
		I G/V PP FP R	
		I G/V PP FP R	
		I G/V PP FP R	
		I G/V PP FP R	
		I G/V PP FP R	
		I G/V PP FP R	
		I G/V PP FP R	
		I G/V PP FP R	
		I G/V PP FP R	
		I G/V PP FP R	
		I G/V PP FP R	
		I G/V PP FP R	

Circle level of prompting using key.

Key:

I = Independent

G/V = Gestural/Verbal

PP = Partial Physical Assistance

FP = Full Partial Assistance

R = Refusal

Show Me the Data! By Leon-Guerrero, Matsumoto, & Martin © 2011. AAPC. www.aapcpublishing.net
SOCIAL – Cooperative Play

Sharing

	Staff:		Date:

Name:

Objective: | **Criteria:**

Date	Peer	Item	Level of Assistance (4,3,2,1,0)	Comments

Record level of assistance using key.

Key:
4 = Independent
3 = Verbal/Gestural
2 = Partial Physical
1 = Full Physical
0 = Refusal

Show Me the Data! By Leon-Guerrero, Matsumoto, & Martin © 2011. AAPC. www.aapcpublishing.net
SOCIAL – Sharing

Turn-Taking		Staff:	Date:

Name:

Objective: **Criteria:**

Date	Level of Assistance	Peer	Item	Comments

Record level of assistance using key.

Key:
4 = Independent
3 = Verbal/Gestural
2 = Partial Physical
1 = Full Physical
0 = Refusal

Show Me the Data! By Leon-Guerrero, Matsumoto, & Martin © 2011. AAPC. www.aapcpublishing.net
SOCIAL – Turn-Taking

A Unique Way to Develop and Implement Meaningful Programs for Students with ASD

The Comprehensive Autism Planning System (CAPS) for Individuals with Asperger Syndrome, Autism and Related Disabilities:
Integrating Best Practices Throughout the Student's Day

Shawn Henry and Brenda Smith Myles, Ph.D.

Code: 9988
Price: $29.95

This comprehensive, yet easy-to-use system allows educators to understand how and when to implement an instructional program for students with autism spectrum disorders (ASD). The CAPS model answers the questions (a) What supports does my student/child need in each class to be successful? (b) What goals is my student/child working on? and (c) Is there a thoughtful sequence to the student's/child's day that matches his learning style. This timely resource addresses adequate yearly progress (AYP), response to intervention (RTI), and positive behavior support (PBS) in a common-sense format. The CAPS process was designed to be used by the child's educational team, consisting of parents, general educators, special educators, paraprofessionals, speech-language pathologists, occupational therapists, physical therapists, administrators, psychologists, consultants, siblings, and others who are stakeholders in the student's education.

The structure of this innovative tool ensures consistent use of supports to ensure student success as well as data collection to measure that success. In addition, CAPS fosters targeted professional development. Because CAPS identifies supports for each of the student's daily activities, it is possible for all educational professionals working with the student to readily identify the methods, supports, and structures in which they themselves need training.

About the authors:

Shawn A. Henry is executive director at the Ohio Center for Autism and Low Incidence (OCALI), where he concentrates on developing statewide change efforts in promoting advances in the training of professionals serving students with autism and providing supports for families. He was previously the program director of training and evaluation at the Kentucky Autism Training Center, University of Louisville (KATC), where he coordinated targeted professional development throughout the state. These experiences, as well as serving as an elementary special education teacher, primarily teaching students with autism, led Mr. Henry to develop the Comprehensive Autism Planning System (CAPS).

Brenda Smith Myles, Ph.D., a consultant with the Ziggurat Group, is the recipient of the 2004 Autism Society of America's Outstanding Professional Award and the 2006 Princeton Fellowship Award. She has written numerous articles and books on Asperger Syndrome and autism, including *Asperger Syndrome and Difficult Moments: Practical Solutions for Tantrums, Rage, and Meltdowns* (with Southwick) and *Asperger Syndrome and Adolescence: Practical Solutions for School Success* (with Adreon). The latter is the winner of the Autism Society of America's 2002 Outstanding Literary Work.

877-277-8254 (toll-free) • www.aapcpublishing.net

AAPC Textbooks

MEETING THE MANDATE FOR HIGHLY QUALIFIED EDUCATORS

AAPC Textbooks Are Classroom-Ready

If you're teaching a college course or preparing for an in-house training, AAPC Textbooks can help. We make the process easy and convenient while adhering to the gold standard in the field by offering with each textbook ...

- Chapter PowerPoint™ Presentations
- Chapter Tests
- Comprehensive Exams
- Case Study Ideas
- Recommendations for In-Class Activities
- Project Ideas
- Paper Topic Ideas
- Supplemental PowerPoint™ Presentations

All support materials are easily tailored to a specific instructor's needs
www.aapctextbooks.net

"My students and I thoroughly enjoyed the Ziggurat book, and in fact, I used it for a second class with the group. It makes so much sense. I used it with the HFA/AS students, but also used the assessment with the classic group . . . I intend to use the Ziggurat again next year for the two courses."

– Deanna Luscre, assistant professor

Intervention

NEW!
Quality Literacy Instruction for Students with Autism Spectrum Disorders

Having effective literacy skills enhances the quality of life of all individuals, including those with autism spectrum disorders. Bringing together experts from both the autism and reading fields, this textbook supports professionals and families alike in building lifelong literacy instruction geared to the needs of students on the autism spectrum. Using case examples, the textbook brings theory and research to practice, thus meeting the mandate for evidence-based practice. ISBN 9781934575666

Edited by Christina Carnahan, Ed.D., and Pam Williamson, Ph.D.; foreword by Kathleen Quill, Ph.D.

Code 9506 (Textbook)   **Price: $59.00**

Foundations/Characteristics

2009 ASA LITERARY WORK OF THE YEAR AWARD!
Learners on the Autism Spectrum: Preparing Highly Qualified Educators

This text responds to the escalating need to prepare highly qualified educators with essential knowledge and practical skills to support diverse learners on the autism spectrum. Covering a range of critical topics and themes, this edited volume brings together leading experts representing diverse disciplines and perspectives (i.e., researchers, therapists, educators, parents, and adults on the autism spectrum) for a comprehensive look at the core issues related to individuals with autism spectrum disorders. ISBN 9781934575079

Edited by Kari Dunn Buron, M.S., and Pamela Wolfberg, Ph.D.; foreword by Carol Gray

Code 9504 (Textbook)   **Price: $59.00**

Intervention Strategies and Comprehensive Planning
BASED ON THE ASA AWARD-WINNING BOOK
Designing Comprehensive Intervention for Individuals with High-Functioning Autism and Asperger Syndrome: The Ziggurat Model

While it is relatively easy to find information describing specific interventions, it is difficult to find information on how to develop a comprehensive intervention plan. This textbook presents a process and framework for designing interventions for individuals of all ages with ASD while staying consistent with recent special education trends, including response to intervention (RTI), evidence-based practices, and positive behavioral supports. ISBN 9781934575093

Ruth Aspy, Ph.D., and Barry Grossman, Ph.D.; foreword by Gary Mesibov, Ph.D.

Code 9502 (Textbook)   **Price: $59.00**

Social Skills Programming
BASED ON THE ASA AWARD-WINNING BOOK
Building Social Relationships: A Systematic Approach to Teaching Social Interaction Skills to Children and Adolescents With Autism Spectrum Disorders and Other Social Difficulties

This textbook addresses the critical need for social skills programming for children and adolescents with autism spectrum disorders and other social difficulties. Unlike other resources, this book presents a comprehensive model that incorporates five fundamental steps: assess social functioning, distinguish between skill acquisition and performance deficits, select intervention strategies, implement intervention, and evaluate and monitor progress. Rather than promoting a single strategy, the model details how to organize and make sense of the myriad social skills programs and resources available. ISBN 9781934575055

Scott Bellini, Ph.D.

Code 9500 (Textbook)   **Price: $59.00**

PUBLISHING

P.O. Box 23173
Shawnee Mission, Kansas 66283-0173
877-277-8254
www.aapcpublishing.net